D0540380

The *Psalms*

of David in Metre

According to
the Version approved by
The Church of Scotland
and appointed to be
used in worship

Trinitarian Bible Soci

Tyndale House, Dorset Road, London, SW19

copyright © 1998 Trinitarian Bible Society

ISBN 1-86228-096-7

Printed and bound in Great Britain by Bath Press

10m/11/02

Psalm 1

1 THAT man hath perfect blessedness
   who walketh not astray
In counsel of ungodly men,
   nor stands in sinners' way,
Nor sitteth in the scorner's chair:
2   But placeth his delight
Upon God's law, and meditates
   on his law day and night.

3 He shall be like a tree that grows
   near planted by a river,
Which in his season yields his fruit,
   and his leaf fadeth never:
And all he doth shall prosper well.
4   The wicked are not so;
But like they are unto the chaff,
   which wind drives to and fro.

5 In judgment therefore shall not stand
   such as ungodly are;
Nor in th' assembly of the just
   shall wicked men appear.
6 For why? the way of godly men
   unto the Lord is known:
Whereas the way of wicked men
   shall quite be overthrown.

Psalm 2

1 WHY rage the heathen? and vain things
   why do the people mind?
2 Kings of the earth do set themselves,
   and princes are combin'd,

To plot against the Lord, and his
    Anointed, saying thus,
3 Let us asunder break their bands,
    and cast their cords from us.

4 He that in heaven sits shall laugh;
    the Lord shall scorn them all.
5 Then shall he speak to them in wrath,
    in rage he vex them shall.
6 Yet, notwithstanding, I have him
    to be my King appointed;
And over Sion, my holy hill,
    I have him King anointed.

7 The sure decree I will declare;
    the Lord hath said to me,
Thou art mine only Son; this day
    I have begotten thee.
8 Ask of me, and for heritage
    the heathen I'll make thine;
And, for possession, I to thee
    will give earth's utmost line.

9 Thou shalt, as with a weighty rod
    of iron, break them all;
And, as a potter's sherd, thou shalt
    them dash in pieces small.
10 Now therefore, kings, be wise; be taught,
    ye judges of the earth:
11 Serve God in fear, and see that ye
    join trembling with your mirth.

12 Kiss ye the Son, lest in his ire
    ye perish from the way,

If once his wrath begin to burn:
    bless'd all that on him stay.

Psalm 3

A Psalm of David, when he fled from Absalom his son.

1 O LORD, how are my foes increas'd?
    against me many rise.
2 Many say of my soul, For him
    in God no succour lies.
3 Yet thou my shield and glory art,
    th' uplifter of mine head.
4 I cry'd, and, from his holy hill,
    the Lord me answer made.

5 I laid me down and slept; I wak'd,
    for God sustained me.
6 I will not fear though thousands ten
    set round against me be.
7 Arise, O Lord; save me, my God;
    for thou my foes hast stroke
  All on the cheek-bone, and the teeth
    of wicked men hast broke.

8 Salvation doth appertain
    unto the Lord alone:
  Thy blessing, Lord, for evermore
    thy people is upon.

Psalm 4

To the chief Musician on Neginoth, A Psalm of David.

1 GIVE ear unto me when I call,
    God of my righteousness;
  Have mercy, hear my pray'r; thou hast
    enlarg'd me in distress.

2 O ye the sons of men! how long
  will ye love vanities?
  How long my glory turn to shame,
  and will ye follow lies?

3 But know, that for himself the Lord
  the godly man doth chuse:
  The Lord, when I on him do call,
  to hear will not refuse.

4 Fear, and sin not; talk with your heart
  on bed, and silent be.

5 Off'rings present of righteousness,
  and in the Lord trust ye.

6 O who will shew us any good?
  is that which many say:
  But of thy countenance the light,
  Lord, lift on us alway.

7 Upon my heart, bestow'd by thee,
  more gladness I have found
  Than they, ev'n then, when corn and wine
  did most with them abound.

8 I will both lay me down in peace,
  and quiet sleep will take;
  Because thou only me to dwell
  in safety, Lord, dost make.

Psalm 5

To the chief Musician upon Nehiloth, A Psalm of David.

1 GIVE ear unto my words, O Lord,
  my meditation weigh.

2 Hear my loud cry, my King, my God;
  for I to thee will pray.

3   Lord, thou shalt early hear my voice:
        I early will direct
    My pray'r to thee; and, looking up,
        an answer will expect.

4   For thou art not a God that doth
        in wickedness delight;
    Neither shall evil dwell with thee,
5   Nor fools stand in thy sight.
    All that ill-doers are thou hat'st;
6   Cutt'st off that liars be:
    The bloody and deceitful man
        abhorred is by thee.

7   But I into thy house will come
        in thine abundant grace;
    And I will worship in thy fear
        toward thy holy place.
8   Because of those mine enemies,
        Lord, in thy righteousness
    Do thou me lead; do thou thy way
        make straight before my face.

9   For in their mouth there is no truth,
        their inward part is ill;
    Their throat's an open sepulchre,
        their tongue doth flatter still.
10 O God, destroy them; let them be
        by their own counsel quell'd:
    Them for their many sins cast out,
        for they 'gainst thee rebell'd.

11 But let all joy that trust in thee,
        and still make shouting noise;

For them thou sav'st: let all that love
    thy name in thee rejoice.
12 For, Lord, unto the righteous man
    thou wilt thy blessing yield:
With favour thou wilt compass him
    about, as with a shield.

Psalm 6

To the chief Musician on Neginoth upon Sheminith,
A Psalm of David.

1 LORD, in thy wrath rebuke me not;
    Nor in thy hot rage chasten me.
2 Lord, pity me, for I am weak:
    Heal me, for my bones vexed be.
3 My soul is also vexed sore;
    But, Lord, how long stay wilt thou make?
4 Return, O Lord, my soul set free;
    O save me, for thy mercies' sake.

5 Because those that deceased are
    Of thee shall no remembrance have;
And who is he that will to thee
    Give praises lying in the grave?
6 I with my groaning weary am,
    I also all the night my bed
Have caused for to swim; and I
    With tears my couch have watered.

7 Mine eye, consum'd with grief, grows old,
    Because of all mine enemies.
8 Hence from me, wicked workers all;
    For God hath heard my weeping cries.
9 God hath my supplication heard,
    My pray'r received graciously.

10 Sham'd and sore vex'd be all my foes,
    Sham'd and back turned suddenly.

Another of the same

1 IN thy great indignation,
    O Lord, rebuke me not;
  Nor on me lay thy chast'ning hand,
    in thy displeasure hot.
2 Lord, I am weak, therefore on me
    have mercy, and me spare:
  Heal me, O Lord, because thou know'st
    my bones much vexed are.

3 My soul is vexed sore: but, Lord,
    how long stay wilt thou make?
4 Return, Lord, free my soul; and save
    me, for thy mercies' sake.
5 Because of thee in death there shall
    no more remembrance be:
  Of those that in the grave do lie,
    who shall give thanks to thee?

6 I with my groaning weary am,
    and all the night my bed
  I caused for to swim; with tears
    my couch I watered.
7 By reason of my vexing grief
    mine eye consumed is;
  It waxeth old, because of all
    that be mine enemies.

8 But now, depart from me all ye
    that work iniquity:
  For why? the Lord hath heard my voice,
    when I did mourn and cry.

9 Unto my supplication
 the Lord did hearing give:
When I to him my prayer make,
 the Lord will it receive.

10 Let all be sham'd and troubled sore,
 That en'mies are to me;
Let them turn back, and suddenly
 ashamed let them be.

Psalm 7

*Shiggaion of David, which he sang unto the Lord,
concerning the words of Cush the Benjamite.*

1 O LORD my God, in thee do I
 my confidence repose:
Save and deliver me from all
 my persecuting foes;
2 Lest that the enemy my soul
 should, like a lion, tear,
In pieces rending it, while there
 is no deliverer.

3 O Lord my God, if it be so
 that I committed this;
If it be so that in my hands
 iniquity there is:
4 If I rewarded ill to him
 that was at peace with me;
(Yea, ev'n the man that without cause
 my foe was I did free;)

5 Then let the foe pursue and take
 my soul, and my life thrust
Down to the earth, and let him lay
 mine honour in the dust.

6   Rise in thy wrath, Lord, raise thyself,
        for my foes raging be;
    And, to the judgment which thou hast
        commanded, wake for me.

7   So shall th' assembly of thy folk
        about encompass thee:
    Thou, therefore, for their sakes, return
        unto thy place on high.
8   The Lord he shall the people judge;
        my judge, JEHOVAH, be,
    After my righteousness, and mine
        integrity in me.

9   O let the wicked's malice end;
        but stablish stedfastly
    The righteous: for the righteous God
        the hearts and reins doth try.
10 In God, who saves th' upright in heart,
        is my defence and stay.
11 God just men judgeth, God is wroth
        with ill men ev'ry day.

12 If he do not return again,
        then he his sword will whet;
    His bow he hath already bent,
        and hath it ready set:
13 He also hath for him prepar'd
        the instruments of death;
    Against the persecutors he
        his shafts ordained hath.

14 Behold, he with iniquity
        doth travail, as in birth;

A mischief he conceived hath,
    and falsehood shall bring forth.
15 He made a pit and digg'd it deep,
    another there to take;
But he is fall'n into the ditch
    which he himself did make.

16 Upon his own head his mischief
    shall be returned home;
His vi'lent dealing also down
    on his own pate shall come.
17 According to his righteousness
    the Lord I'll magnify;
And will sing praise unto the name
    of God that is most high.

Psalm 8

To the chief Musician upon Gittith,
A Psalm of David.

1 HOW excellent in all the earth,
    Lord, our Lord, is thy name!
Who hast thy glory far advanc'd
    above the starry frame.
2 From infants' and from sucklings' mouth
    thou didest strength ordain,
For thy foes' cause, that so thou might'st
    th' avenging foe restrain.

3 When I look up unto the heav'ns,
    which thine own fingers fram'd,
Unto the moon, and to the stars,
    which were by thee ordain'd;
4 Then say I, What is man, that he
    remember'd is by thee?

Or what the son of man, that thou
    so kind to him should'st be?

5 For thou a little lower hast
    him than the angels made;
  With glory and with dignity
    thou crowned hast his head.
6 Of thy hands' works thou mad'st him lord,
    all under's feet didst lay;
7 All sheep and oxen, yea, and beasts
    that in the field do stray;

8 Fowls of the air, fish of the sea,
    all that pass through the same.
9 How excellent in all the earth,
    Lord, our Lord, is thy name!

Psalm 9

To the chief Musician upon Muth-labben,
A Psalm of David.

1 LORD, thee I'll praise with all my heart,
    thy wonders all proclaim.
2 In thee, most High, I'll greatly joy,
    and sing unto thy name.
3 When back my foes were turn'd, they fell,
    and perish'd at thy sight:
4 For thou maintain'dst my right and cause;
    on throne sat'st judging right.

5 The heathen thou rebuked hast,
    the wicked overthrown;
  Thou hast put out their names, that they
    may never more be known.
6 O en'my! now destructions have
    an end perpetual:

Thou cities raz'd; perish'd with them
 is their memorial.

7 God shall endure for aye; he doth
  for judgment set his throne;
8 In righteousness to judge the world,
  justice to give each one.
9 God also will a refuge be
  for those that are oppress'd;
 A refuge will he be in times
  of trouble to distress'd.

10 And they that know thy name, in thee
  their confidence will place:
 For thou hast not forsaken them
  that truly seek thy face.
11 O sing ye praises to the Lord
  that dwells in Sion hill;
 And all the nations among
  his deeds record ye still.

12 When he enquireth after blood,
  he then rememb'reth them:
 The humble folk he not forgets
  that call upon his name.
13 Lord, pity me; behold the grief
  which I from foes sustain;
 Ev'n thou, who from the gates of death
  dost raise me up again;

14 That I, in Sion's daughters' gates,
  may all thy praise advance;
 And that I may rejoice always
  in thy deliverance.

15 The heathen are sunk in the pit
   which they themselves prepar'd;
And in the net which they have hid
   their own feet fast are snar'd.

16 The Lord is by the judgment known
   which he himself hath wrought:
The sinners' hands do make the snares
   wherewith themselves are caught.
17 They who are wicked into hell
   each one shall turned be;
And all the nations that forget
   to seek the Lord most high.

18 For they that needy are shall not
   forgotten be alway;
The expectation of the poor
   shall not be lost for aye.
19 Arise, Lord, let not man prevail;
   judge heathen in thy sight:
20 That they may know themselves but men,
   the nations, Lord, affright.

Psalm 10

1 WHEREFORE is it that thou, O Lord,
   dost stand from us afar?
And wherefore hidest thou thyself
   when times so troublous are?
2 The wicked in his loftiness
   doth persecute the poor:
In these devices they have fram'd
   let them be taken sure.

3   The wicked of his heart's desire
      doth talk with boasting great;
    He blesseth him that's covetous,
      whom yet the Lord doth hate.
4   The wicked, through his pride of face,
      on God he doth not call;
    And in the counsels of his heart
      the Lord is not at all.

5   His ways they always grievous are;
      thy judgments from his sight
    Removed are: at all his foes
      he puffeth with despite.
6   Within his heart he thus hath said,
      I shall not moved be;
    And no adversity at all
      shall ever come to me.

7   His mouth with cursing, fraud, deceit,
      is fill'd abundantly;
    And underneath his tongue there is
      mischief and vanity.
8   He closely sits in villages;
      he slays the innocent:
    Against the poor that pass him by
      his cruel eyes are bent.

9   He, lion-like, lurks in his den;
      he waits the poor to take;
    And when he draws him in his net,
      his prey he doth him make.
10 Himself he humbleth very low,
      he croucheth down withal,
    That so a multitude of poor
      may by his strong ones fall.

11 He thus hath said within his heart,
    The Lord hath quite forgot;
He hides his countenance, and he
    for ever sees it not.
12 O Lord, do thou arise; O God,
    lift up thine hand on high:
Put not the meek afflicted ones
    out of thy memory.

13 Why is it that the wicked man
    thus doth the Lord despise?
Because that God will it require
    he in his heart denies.
14 Thou hast it seen; for their mischief
    and spite thou wilt repay:
The poor commits himself to thee;
    thou art the orphan's stay.

15 The arm break of the wicked man,
    and of the evil one;
Do thou seek out his wickedness,
    until thou findest none.
16 The Lord is king through ages all,
    ev'n to eternity;
The heathen people from his land
    are perish'd utterly.

17 O Lord, of those that humble are
    thou the desire didst hear;
Thou wilt prepare their heart, and thou
    to hear wilt bend thine ear;
18 To judge the fatherless, and those
    that are oppressed sore;
That man, that is but sprung of earth,
    may them oppress no more.

Psalm 11

To the chief Musician, A Psalm of David.

1 I IN the Lord do put my trust;
    how is it then that ye
Say to my soul, Flee, as a bird,
    unto your mountain high?
2 For, lo, the wicked bend their bow,
    their shafts on string they fit,
That those who upright are in heart
    they privily may hit.

3 If the foundations be destroy'd,
    what hath the righteous done?
4 God in his holy temple is,
    in heaven is his throne:
His eyes do see, his eyelids try
5   men's sons. The just he proves:
But his soul hates the wicked man,
    and him that vi'lence loves.

6 Snares, fire and brimstone, furious storms,
    on sinners he shall rain:
This, as the portion of their cup,
    doth unto them pertain.
7 Because the Lord most righteous doth
    in righteousness delight;
And with a pleasant countenance
    beholdeth the upright.

Psalm 12

To the chief Musician upon Sheminith, A Psalm of David.

1 HELP, Lord, because the godly man
    doth daily fade away;

And from among the sons of men
    the faithful do decay.
2   Unto his neighbour ev'ry one
    doth utter vanity:
They with a double heart do speak,
    and lips of flattery.

3   God shall cut off all flatt'ring lips,
    tongues that speak proudly thus,
4   We'll with our tongue prevail, our lips
    are ours: who's lord o'er us?
5   For poor oppress'd, and for the sighs
    of needy, rise will I,
Saith God, and him in safety set
    from such as him defy.

6   The words of God are words most pure;
    they be like silver try'd
In earthen furnace, seven times
    that hath been purify'd.
7   Lord, thou shalt them preserve and keep
    for ever from this race.
8   On each side walk the wicked, when
    vile men are high in place.

Psalm 13

To the chief Musician, A Psalm of David.

1   HOW long wilt thou forget me, Lord?
    shall it for ever be?
O how long shall it be that thou
    wilt hide thy face from me?
2   How long take counsel in my soul,
    still sad in heart, shall I?

How long exalted over me
    shall be mine enemy?

3 O Lord my God, consider well,
    and answer to me make:
  Mine eyes enlighten, lest the sleep
    of death me overtake:
4 Lest that mine enemy should say,
    Against him I prevail'd;
  And those that trouble me rejoice,
    when I am mov'd and fail'd.

5 But I have all my confidence
    thy mercy set upon;
  My heart within me shall rejoice
    in thy salvation.
6 I will unto the Lord my God
    sing praises cheerfully,
  Because he hath his bounty shown
    to me abundantly.

Psalm 14

To the chief Musician, A Psalm of David.

1 THAT there is not a God, the fool
    doth in his heart conclude:
  They are corrupt, their works are vile;
    not one of them doth good.
2 Upon men's sons the Lord from heav'n
    did cast his eyes abroad,
  To see if any understood,
    and did seek after God.

3 They altogether filthy are,
    they all aside are gone;

And there is none that doeth good,
    yea, sure there is not one.
4 These workers of iniquity
    do they not know at all,
That they my people eat as bread,
    and on God do not call?

5 There fear'd they much; for God is with
    the whole race of the just.
6 You shame the counsel of the poor,
    because God is his trust.
7 Let Isr'el's help from Sion come:
    when back the Lord shall bring
His captives, Jacob shall rejoice,
    and Israel shall sing.

Psalm 15

A Psalm of David.

1 WITHIN thy tabernacle, Lord,
    who shall abide with thee?
And in thy high and holy hill
    who shall a dweller be?
2 The man that walketh uprightly,
    and worketh righteousness,
And as he thinketh in his heart,
    so doth he truth express.

3 Who doth not slander with his tongue,
    nor to his friend doth hurt;
Nor yet against his neighbour doth
    take up an ill report.
4 In whose eyes vile men are despis'd;
    but those that God do fear

He honoureth; and changeth not,
    though to his hurt he swear.

5   His coin puts not to usury,
      nor take reward will he
Against the guiltless. Who doth thus
    shall never moved be.

Psalm 16

Michtam of David.

1   LORD, keep me; for I trust in thee.
2   To God thus was my speech,
Thou art my Lord; and unto thee
    my goodness doth not reach:
3   To saints on earth, to th' excellent,
      where my delight's all plac'd.
4   Their sorrows shall be multiply'd
      to other gods that haste:

Of their drink-offerings of blood
    I will no off'ring make;
Yea, neither I their very names
    up in my lips will take.
5   God is of mine inheritance
      and cup the portion;
The lot that fallen is to me
    thou dost maintain alone.

6   Unto me happily the lines
      in pleasant places fell;
Yea, the inheritance I got
    in beauty doth excel.
7   I bless the Lord, because he doth
      by counsel me conduct;

And in the seasons of the night
   my reins do me instruct.

8   Before me still the Lord I set:
     sith it is so that he
Doth ever stand at my right hand,
     I shall not moved be.
9   Because of this my heart is glad,
     and joy shall be exprest
Ev'n by my glory; and my flesh
     in confidence shall rest.

10 Because my soul in grave to dwell
     shall not be left by thee;
Nor wilt thou give thine Holy One
     corruption to see.
11 Thou wilt me shew the path of life:
     of joys there is full store
Before thy face; at thy right hand
     are pleasures evermore.

Psalm 17

A Prayer of David.

1   L ORD, hear the right, attend my cry,
     unto my pray'r give heed,
That doth not in hypocrisy
     from feigned lips proceed.
2   And from before thy presence forth
     my sentence do thou send:
Toward these things that equal are
     do thou thine eyes intend.

3   Thou prov'dst mine heart, thou visit'dst me
     by night, thou didst me try,

Yet nothing found'st; for that my mouth
    shall not sin, purpos'd I.
4 As for men's works, I, by the word
    that from thy lips doth flow,
Did me preserve out of the paths
    wherein destroyers go.

5 Hold up my goings, Lord, me guide
    in those thy paths divine,
So that my footsteps may not slide
    out of those ways of thine.
6 I called have on thee, O God,
    because thou wilt me hear:
That thou may'st hearken to my speech,
    to me incline thine ear.

7 Thy wondrous loving-kindness show,
    thou that, by thy right hand,
Sav'st them that trust in thee from those
    that up against them stand.
8 As th' apple of the eye me keep;
    in thy wings' shade me close
9 From lewd oppressors, compassing
    me round, as deadly foes.

10 In their own fat they are inclos'd;
    their mouth speaks loftily.
11 Our steps they compass'd; and to ground
    down bowing set their eye.
12 He like unto a lion is
    that's greedy of his prey,
Or lion young, which lurking doth
    in secret places stay.

13 Arise, and disappoint my foe,
 and cast him down, O Lord:
My soul save from the wicked man,
 the man which is thy sword.
14 From men, which are thy hand, O Lord,
 from worldly men me save,
Which only in this present life
 their part and portion have.

Whose belly with thy treasure hid
 thou fill'st: they children have
In plenty; of their goods the rest
 they to their children leave.
15 But as for me, I thine own face
 in righteousness will see;
And with thy likeness, when I wake,
 I satisfy'd shall be.

Psalm 18

*To the chief Musician, A Psalm of David, the servant of the Lord,
who spake unto the Lord the words of this song in the day
that the Lord delivered him from the hand of all his enemies,
and from the hand of Saul: And he said,*

1 THEE will I love, O Lord, my strength.
2   My fortress is the Lord,
My rock, and he that doth to me
 deliverance afford:
My God, my strength, whom I will trust,
 a buckler unto me,
The horn of my salvation,
 and my high tow'r, is he.

3 Upon the Lord, who worthy is
 of praises, will I cry;

And then shall I preserved be
  safe from mine enemy.
4 Floods of ill men affrighted me,
   death's pangs about me went;
5 Hell's sorrows me environed;
   death's snares did me prevent.

6 In my distress I call'd on God,
   cry to my God did I;
  He from his temple heard my voice,
   to his ears came my cry.
7 Th' earth, as affrighted, then did shake,
   trembling upon it seiz'd:
  The hills' foundations moved were,
   because he was displeas'd.

8 Up from his nostrils came a smoke,
   and from his mouth there came
  Devouring fire, and coals by it
   were turned into flame.
9 He also bowed down the heav'ns,
   and thence he did descend;
  And thickest clouds of darkness did
   under his feet attend.

10 And he upon a cherub rode,
   and thereon he did fly;
  Yea, on the swift wings of the wind
   his flight was from on high.
11 He darkness made his secret place:
   about him, for his tent,
  Dark waters were, and thickest clouds
   of th' airy firmament.

12 And at the brightness of that light,
    which was before his eye,
His thick clouds pass'd away, hailstones
    and coals of fire did fly.
13 The Lord God also in the heav'ns
    did thunder in his ire;
And there the Highest gave his voice,
    hailstones and coals of fire.

14 Yea, he his arrows sent abroad,
    and them he scattered;
His lightnings also he shot out,
    and them discomfited.
15 The waters' channels then were seen,
    the world's foundations vast
At thy rebuke discover'd were,
    and at thy nostrils' blast.

16 And from above the Lord sent down,
    and took me from below;
From many waters he me drew,
    which would me overflow.
17 He me reliev'd from my strong foes,
    and such as did me hate;
Because he saw that they for me
    too strong were, and too great.

18 They me prevented in the day
    of my calamity;
But even then the Lord himself
    a stay was unto me.
19 He to a place where liberty
    and room was hath me brought;

Because he took delight in me,
    he my deliv'rance wrought.

20 According to my righteousness
    he did me recompense,
He me repaid according to
    my hands' pure innocence.
21 For I God's ways kept, from my God
    did not turn wickedly.
22 His judgments were before me, I
    his laws put not from me.

23 Sincere before him was my heart,
    with him upright was I;
And watchfully I kept myself
    from mine iniquity.
24 After my righteousness the Lord
    hath recompensed me,
After the cleanness of my hands
    appearing in his eye.

25 Thou gracious to the gracious art,
    to upright men upright:
26 Pure to the pure, froward thou kyth'st
    unto the froward wight.
27 For thou wilt the afflicted save
    in grief that low do lie:
But wilt bring down the countenance
    of them whose looks are high.

28 The Lord will light my candle so,
    that it shall shine full bright:
The Lord my God will also make
    my darkness to be light.

29 By thee through troops of men I break,
    and them discomfit all;
And, by my God assisting me,
    I overleap a wall.

30 As for God, perfect is his way:
    the Lord his word is try'd;
He is a buckler to all those
    who do in him confide.
31 Who but the Lord is God? but he
    who is a rock and stay?
32 'Tis God that girdeth me with strength,
    and perfect makes my way.

33 He made my feet swift as the hinds,
    set me on my high places.
34 Mine hands to war he taught, mine arms
    brake bows of steel in pieces.
35 The shield of thy salvation
    thou didst on me bestow:
Thy right hand held me up, and great
    thy kindness made me grow.

36 And in my way my steps thou hast
    enlarged under me,
That I go safely, and my feet
    are kept from sliding free.
37 Mine en'mies I pursued have,
    and did them overtake;
Nor did I turn again till I
    an end of them did make.

38 I wounded them, they could not rise;
    they at my feet did fall.

39 Thou girdedst me with strength for war;
    my foes thou brought'st down all:
40 And thou hast giv'n to me the necks
    of all mine enemies;
That I might them destroy and slay,
    who did against me rise.

41 They cried out, but there was none
    that would or could them save;
Yea, they did cry unto the Lord,
    but he no answer gave.
42 Then did I beat them small as dust
    before the wind that flies;
And I did cast them out like dirt
    upon the street that lies.

43 Thou mad'st me free from people's strife,
    and heathen's head to be:
A people whom I have not known
    shall service do to me.
44 At hearing they shall me obey,
    to me they shall submit.
45 Strangers for fear shall fade away,
    who in close places sit.

46 God lives, bless'd be my Rock; the God
    of my health praised be.
47 God doth avenge me, and subdues
    the people under me.
48 He saves me from mine enemies;
    yea, thou hast lifted me
Above my foes; and from the man
    of vi'lence set me free.

49 Therefore to thee will I give thanks
    the heathen folk among;
And to thy name, O Lord, I will
    sing praises in a song.
50 He great deliv'rance gives his king:
    he mercy doth extend
To David, his anointed one,
    and his seed without end.

Psalm 19

To the chief Musician, A Psalm of David.

1 THE heav'ns God's glory do declare,
    the skies his hand-works preach:
2 Day utters speech to day, and night
    to night doth knowledge teach.
3 There is no speech nor tongue to which
    their voice doth not extend:
4 Their line is gone through all the earth,
    their words to the world's end.

In them he set the sun a tent;
5   Who, bridegroom-like, forth goes
From's chamber, as a strong man doth
    to run his race rejoice.
6 From heav'n's end is his going forth,
    circling to th' end again;
And there is nothing from his heat
    that hidden doth remain.

7 God's law is perfect, and converts
    the soul in sin that lies:
God's testimony is most sure,
    and makes the simple wise.

8 The statutes of the Lord are right,
   and do rejoice the heart:
   The Lord's command is pure, and doth
   light to the eyes impart.

9 Unspotted is the fear of God,
   and doth endure for ever:
   The judgments of the Lord are true
   and righteous altogether.
10 They more than gold, yea, much fine gold,
   to be desired are:
   Than honey, honey from the comb
   that droppeth, sweeter far.

11 Moreover, they thy servant warn
   how he his life should frame:
   A great reward provided is
   for them that keep the same.
12 Who can his errors understand?
   O cleanse thou me within
13 From secret faults. Thy servant keep
   from all presumptuous sin:

   And do not suffer them to have
   dominion over me:
   Then, righteous and innocent,
   I from much sin shall be.
14 The words which from my mouth proceed,
   the thoughts sent from my heart,
   Accept, O Lord, for thou my strength
   and my Redeemer art.

Psalm 20

To the chief Musician, A Psalm of David.

1 JEHOVAH hear thee in the day
 when trouble he doth send:
 And let the name of Jacob's God
  thee from all ill defend.
2 O let him help send from above,
 out of his sanctuary:
 From Sion, his own holy hill,
  let him give strength to thee.

3 Let him remember all thy gifts,
 accept thy sacrifice:
4 Grant thee thine heart's wish, and fulfil
 thy thoughts and counsel wise.
5 In thy salvation we will joy;
 in our God's name we will
 Display our banners: and the Lord
  thy prayers all fulfil.

6 Now know I God his king doth save:
 he from his holy heav'n
 Will hear him, with the saving strength
  by his own right hand giv'n.
7 In chariots some put confidence,
 some horses trust upon:
 But we remember will the name
  of our Lord God alone.

8 We rise, and upright stand, when they
 are bowed down, and fall.
9 Deliver, Lord; and let the King
 us hear, when we do call.

Psalm 21

To the chief Musician, A Psalm of David.

1 THE king in thy great strength, O Lord,
    shall very joyful be:
In thy salvation rejoice
    how veh'mently shall he!
2 Thou hast bestowed upon him
    all that his heart would have;
And thou from him didst not withhold
    whate'er his lips did crave.

3 For thou with blessings him prevent'st
    of goodness manifold;
And thou hast set upon his head
    a crown of purest gold.
4 When he desired life of thee,
    thou life to him didst give;
Ev'n such a length of days, that he
    for evermore should live.

5 In that salvation wrought by thee
    his glory is made great;
Honour and comely majesty
    thou hast upon him set.
6 Because that thou for evermore
    most blessed hast him made;
And thou hast with thy countenance
    made him exceeding glad.

7 Because the king upon the Lord
    his confidence doth lay;
And through the grace of the most High
    shall not be mov'd away.

8   Thine hand shall all those men find out
       that en'mies are to thee;
    Ev'n thy right hand shall find out those
       of thee that haters be.

9   Like fiery ov'n thou shalt them make,
       when kindled is thine ire;
    God shall them swallow in his wrath,
       devour them shall the fire.

10 Their fruit from earth thou shalt destroy,
       their seed men from among:
11 For they beyond their might 'gainst thee
       did plot mischief and wrong.

12 Thou therefore shalt make them turn back,
       when thou thy shafts shalt place
    Upon thy strings, made ready all
       to fly against their face.
13 In thy great pow'r and strength, O Lord,
       be thou exalted high;
    So shall we sing with joyful hearts,
       thy power praise shall we.

Psalm 22

To the chief Musician upon Aijeleth Shahar, A Psalm of David.

1   MY God, my God, why hast thou me
       forsaken? why so far
    Art thou from helping me, and from
       my words that roaring are?
2   All day, my God, to thee I cry,
       yet am not heard by thee;
    And in the season of the night
       I cannot silent be.

3   But thou art holy, thou that dost
        inhabit Isr'el's praise.
4   Our fathers hop'd in thee, they hop'd,
        and thou didst them release.
5   When unto thee they sent their cry,
        to them deliv'rance came:
    Because they put their trust in thee,
        they were not put to shame.

6   But as for me, a worm I am,
        and as no man am priz'd:
    Reproach of men I am, and by
        the people am despis'd.
7   All that me see laugh me to scorn;
        shoot out the lip do they;
    They nod and shake their heads at me,
        and, mocking, thus do say,

8   This man did trust in God, that he
        would free him by his might:
    Let him deliver him, sith he
        had in him such delight.
9   But thou art he out of the womb
        that didst me safely take;
    When I was on my mother's breasts
        thou me to hope didst make.

10   And I was cast upon thy care,
        ev'n from the womb till now;
    And from my mother's belly, Lord,
        my God and guide art thou.
11   Be not far off, for grief is near,
        and none to help is found.

12 Bulls many compass me, strong bulls
    of Bashan me surround.

13 Their mouths they open'd wide on me,
    upon me gape did they,
  Like to a lion ravening
    and roaring for his prey.
14 Like water I'm pour'd out, my bones
    all out of joint do part:
  Amidst my bowels, as the wax,
    so melted is my heart.

15 My strength is like a potsherd dry'd;
    my tongue it cleaveth fast
  Unto my jaws; and to the dust
    of death thou brought me hast.
16 For dogs have compass'd me about:
    the wicked, that did meet
  In their assembly, me inclos'd;
    they pierc'd my hands and feet.

17 I all my bones may tell; they do
    upon me look and stare.
18 Upon my vesture lots they cast,
    and clothes among them share.
19 But be not far, O Lord, my strength;
    haste to give help to me.
20 From sword my soul, from pow'r of dogs
    my darling set thou free.

21 Out of the roaring lion's mouth
    do thou me shield and save:
  For from the horns of unicorns
    an ear to me thou gave.

22 I will shew forth thy name unto
    those that my brethren are;
Amidst the congregation
    thy praise I will declare.

23 Praise ye the Lord, who do him fear;
    him glorify all ye
The seed of Jacob; fear him all
    that Isr'el's children be.
24 For he despis'd not nor abhorr'd
    th' afflicted's misery;
Nor from him hid his face, but heard
    when he to him did cry.

25 Within the congregation great
    my praise shall be of thee;
My vows before them that him fear
    shall be perform'd by me.
26 The meek shall eat, and shall be fill'd;
    they also praise shall give
Unto the Lord that do him seek:
    your heart shall ever live.

27 All ends of th' earth remember shall,
    and turn the Lord unto;
All kindreds of the nations
    to him shall homage do:
28 Because the kingdom to the Lord
    doth appertain as his;
Likewise among the nations
    the Governor he is.

29 Earth's fat ones eat, and worship shall:
    all who to dust descend

Shall bow to him; none of them can
   his soul from death defend.
30 A seed shall service do to him;
   unto the Lord it shall
Be for a generation
   reckon'd in ages all.

31 They shall come, and they shall declare
   his truth and righteousness
Unto a people yet unborn,
   and that he hath done this.

Psalm 23

A Psalm of David.

1 THE Lord's my shepherd, I'll not want.
2   He makes me down to lie
In pastures green: he leadeth me
   the quiet waters by.
3 My soul he doth restore again;
   and me to walk doth make
Within the paths of righteousness,
   ev'n for his own name's sake.

4 Yea, though I walk in death's dark vale,
   yet will I fear none ill:
For thou art with me; and thy rod
   and staff me comfort still.
5 My table thou hast furnished
   in presence of my foes;
My head thou dost with oil anoint,
   and my cup overflows.

6 Goodness and mercy all my life
   shall surely follow me:

And in God's house for evermore
my dwelling-place shall be.

Psalm 24
A Psalm of David.

1   THE earth belongs unto the Lord,
and all that it contains;
The world that is inhabited,
and all that there remains.

2   For the foundations thereof
he on the seas did lay,
And he hath it established
upon the floods to stay.

3   Who is the man that shall ascend
into the hill of God?
Or who within his holy place
shall have a firm abode?

4   Whose hands are clean, whose heart is pure,
and unto vanity
Who hath not lifted up his soul,
nor sworn deceitfully.

5   He from th' Eternal shall receive
the blessing him upon,
And righteousness, ev'n from the God
of his salvation.

6   This is the generation
that after him enquire,
O Jacob, who do seek thy face
with their whole heart's desire.

7   Ye gates, lift up your heads on high;
ye doors that last for aye,

Be lifted up, that so the King
   of glory enter may.
8 But who of glory is the King?
    The mighty Lord is this;
   Ev'n that same Lord, that great in might
    and strong in battle is.

9 Ye gates, lift up your heads; ye doors,
    doors that do last for aye,
   Be lifted up, that so the King
    of glory enter may.
10 But who is he that is the King
    of glory? who is this?
   The Lord of hosts, and none but he,
    the King of glory is.

Psalm 25

A Psalm of David.

1 TO thee I lift my soul:
2   O Lord, I trust in thee:
   My God, let me not be asham'd,
    nor foes triumph o'er me.
3 Let none that wait on thee
    be put to shame at all;
   But those that without cause transgress,
    let shame upon them fall.

4 Shew me thy ways, O Lord;
    thy paths, O teach thou me:
5 And do thou lead me in thy truth,
    therein my teacher be:
   For thou art God that dost
    to me salvation send,

And I upon thee all the day
  expecting do attend.

6 Thy tender mercies, Lord,
    I pray thee to remember,
And loving-kindnesses; for they
  have been of old for ever.
7 My sins and faults of youth
    do thou, O Lord, forget:
After thy mercy think on me,
  and for thy goodness great.

8 God good and upright is:
    the way he'll sinners show.
9 The meek in judgment he will guide,
    and make his path to know.
10 The whole paths of the Lord
    are truth and mercy sure,
To those that do his cov'nant keep,
  and testimonies pure.

11 Now, for thine own name's sake,
    O Lord, I thee entreat
To pardon mine iniquity;
  for it is very great.
12 What man is he that fears
    the Lord, and doth him serve?
Him shall he teach the way that he
  shall choose, and still observe.

13 His soul shall dwell at ease;
    and his posterity
Shall flourish still, and of the earth
  inheritors shall be.

14 With those that fear him is
    the secret of the Lord;
  The knowledge of his covenant
    he will to them afford.

15 Mine eyes upon the Lord
    continually are set;
  For he it is that shall bring forth
    my feet out of the net.
16 Turn unto me thy face,
    and to me mercy show;
  Because that I am desolate,
    and am brought very low.

17 My heart's griefs are increas'd:
    me from distress relieve.
18 See mine affliction and my pain,
    and all my sins forgive.
19 Consider thou my foes,
    because they many are;
  And it a cruel hatred is
    which they against me bear.

20 O do thou keep my soul,
    do thou deliver me:
  And let me never be asham'd,
    because I trust in thee.
21 Let uprightness and truth
    keep me, who thee attend.
22 Redemption, Lord, to Israel
    from all his troubles send.

Another of the same

1 TO thee I lift my soul, O Lord:
2   My God, I trust in thee:
  Let me not be asham'd; let not
      my foes triumph o'er me.
3 Yea, let thou none ashamed be
      that do on thee attend:
  Ashamed let them be, O Lord,
      who without cause offend.

4 Thy ways, Lord, shew; teach me thy paths:
5   Lead me in truth, teach me:
  For of my safety thou art God;
      all day I wait on thee.
6 Thy mercies, that most tender are,
      do thou, O Lord, remember,
  And loving-kindnesses; for they
      have been of old for ever.

7 Let not the errors of my youth,
      nor sins, remember'd be:
  In mercy, for thy goodness' sake,
      O Lord, remember me.
8 The Lord is good and gracious,
      he upright is also:
  He therefore sinners will instruct
      in ways that they should go.

9 The meek and lowly he will guide
      in judgment just alway:
  To meek and poor afflicted ones
      he'll clearly teach his way.
10 The whole paths of the Lord our God
      are truth and mercy sure,

To such as keep his covenant,
  and testimonies pure.

11 Now, for thine own name's sake, O Lord,
    I humbly thee entreat
  To pardon mine iniquity;
    for it is very great.
12 What man fears God? him shall he teach
    the way that he shall chuse.
13 His soul shall dwell at ease; his seed
    the earth, as heirs, shall use.

14 The secret of the Lord is with
    such as do fear his name;
  And he his holy covenant
    will manifest to them.
15 Towards the Lord my waiting eyes
    continually are set;
  For he it is that shall bring forth
    my feet out of the net.

16 O turn thee unto me, O God,
    have mercy me upon;
  Because I solitary am,
    and in affliction.
17 Enlarg'd the griefs are of mine heart;
    me from distress relieve.
18 See mine affliction and my pain,
    and all my sins forgive.

19 Consider thou mine enemies,
    because they many are;
  And it a cruel hatred is
    which they against me bear.

20 O do thou keep my soul; O God,
  do thou deliver me:
Let me not be asham'd; for I
  do put my trust in thee.

21 O let integrity and truth
  keep me, who thee attend.
22 Redemption, Lord, to Israel
  from all his troubles send.

Psalm 26

A Psalm of David.

1 JUDGE me, O Lord, for I have walk'd
  in mine integrity:
I trusted also in the Lord;
  slide therefore shall not I.
2 Examine me, and do me prove;
  try heart and reins, O God:
3 For thy love is before mine eyes,
  thy truth's paths I have trode.

4 With persons vain I have not sat,
  nor with dissemblers gone:
5 Th' assembly of ill men I hate;
  to sit with such I shun.
6 Mine hands in innocence, O Lord,
  I'll wash and purify;
So to thine holy altar go,
  and compass it will I:

7 That I, with voice of thanksgiving,
  may publish and declare,

And tell of all thy mighty works,
    that great and wondrous are.
8   The habitation of thy house,
    Lord, I have loved well;
    Yea, in that place I do delight
    where doth thine honour dwell.

9   With sinners gather not my soul,
    and such as blood would spill:
10   Whose hands mischievous plots, right hand
    corrupting bribes do fill.
11   But as for me, I will walk on
    in mine integrity:
    Do thou redeem me, and, O Lord,
    be merciful to me.

12   My foot upon an even place
    doth stand with stedfastness:
    Within the congregations
    th' Eternal I will bless.

Psalm 27

A Psalm of David.

1   THE Lord's my light and saving health,
    who shall make me dismay'd?
    My life's strength is the Lord, of whom
    then shall I be afraid?
2   When as mine enemies and foes,
    most wicked persons all,
    To eat my flesh against me rose,
    they stumbled and did fall.

3   Against me though an host encamp,
    my heart yet fearless is:

Though war against me rise, I will
    be confident in this.
4 One thing I of the Lord desir'd,
    and will seek to obtain,
That all days of my life I may
    within God's house remain;

That I the beauty of the Lord
    behold may and admire,
And that I in his holy place
    may rev'rently enquire.
5 For he in his pavilion shall
    me hide in evil days;
In secret of his tent me hide,
    and on a rock me raise.

6 And now, ev'n at this present time,
    mine head shall lifted be
Above all those that are my foes,
    and round encompass me:
Therefore unto his tabernacle
    I'll sacrifices bring
Of joyfulness; I'll sing, yea, I
    to God will praises sing.

7 O Lord, give ear unto my voice,
    when I do cry to thee;
Upon me also mercy have,
    and do thou answer me.
8 When thou didst say, Seek ye my face,
    then unto thee reply
Thus did my heart, Above all things
    thy face, Lord, seek will I.

9 Far from me hide not thou thy face;
     put not away from thee
    Thy servant in thy wrath: thou hast
     an helper been to me.
    O God of my salvation,
     leave me not, nor forsake:
10 Though me my parents both should leave,
     the Lord will me up take.

11 O Lord, instruct me in thy way,
     to me a leader be
    In a plain path, because of those
     that hatred bear to me.
12 Give me not to mine en'mies' will;
     for witnesses that lie
    Against me risen are, and such
     as breathe out cruelty.

13 I fainted had, unless that I
     believed had to see
    The Lord's own goodness in the land
     of them that living be.
14 Wait on the Lord, and be thou strong,
     and he shall strength afford
    Unto thine heart; yea, do thou wait,
     I say, upon the Lord.

Psalm 28

A Psalm of David.

1 TO thee I'll cry, O Lord, my rock;
     hold not thy peace to me;
    Lest like those that to pit descend
     I by thy silence be.

2   The voice hear of my humble pray'rs,
         when unto thee I cry;
     When to thine holy oracle
         I lift mine hands on high.

3   With ill men draw me not away
         that work iniquity;
     That speak peace to their friends, while in
         their hearts doth mischief lie.
4   Give them according to their deeds
         and ills endeavoured:
     And as their handy-works deserve,
         to them be rendered.

5   God shall not build, but them destroy,
         who would not understand
     The Lord's own works, nor did regard
         the doing of his hand.
6   For ever blessed be the Lord,
         for graciously he heard
     The voice of my petitions,
         and prayers did regard.

7   The Lord's my strength and shield; my heart
         upon him did rely;
     And I am helped: hence my heart
         doth joy exceedingly,
     And with my song I will him praise.
8   Their strength is God alone:
     He also is the saving strength
         of his anointed one.

9   O thine own people do thou save,
         bless thine inheritance;

Them also do thou feed, and them
 for evermore advance.

Psalm 29

A Psalm of David.

1 GIVE ye unto the Lord, ye sons
  that of the mighty be,
 All strength and glory to the Lord
  with cheerfulness give ye.
2 Unto the Lord the glory give
  that to his name is due;
 And in the beauty of holiness
  unto JEHOVAH bow.

3 The Lord's voice on the waters is;
  the God of majesty
 Doth thunder, and on multitudes
  of waters sitteth he.
4 A pow'rful voice it is that comes
  out from the Lord most high;
 The voice of that great Lord is full
  of glorious majesty.

5 The voice of the Eternal doth
  asunder cedars tear;
 Yea, God the Lord doth cedars break
  that Lebanon doth bear.
6 He makes them like a calf to skip,
  ev'n that great Lebanon,
 And, like to a young unicorn,
  the mountain Sirion.

7 God's voice divides the flames of fire;
8 The desert it doth shake:

The Lord doth make the wilderness
    of Kadesh all to quake.
9 God's voice doth make the hinds to calve,
    it makes the forest bare:
And in his temple ev'ry one
    his glory doth declare.

10 The Lord sits on the floods; the Lord
    sits King, and ever shall.
11 The Lord will give his people strength,
    and with peace bless them all.

Psalm 30

A Psalm and Song at the dedication of the house of David.

1 L ORD, I will thee extol, for thou
    hast lifted me on high,
And over me thou to rejoice
    mad'st not mine enemy.
2 O thou who art the Lord my God,
    I in distress to thee,
With loud cries lifted up my voice,
    and thou hast healed me.

3 O Lord, my soul thou hast brought up,
    and rescu'd from the grave;
That I to pit should not go down,
    alive thou didst me save.
4 O ye that are his holy ones,
    sing praise unto the Lord;
And give unto him thanks, when ye
    his holiness record.

5 For but a moment lasts his wrath;
    life in his favour lies:

Weeping may for a night endure,
    at morn doth joy arise.
6 In my prosperity I said,
    that nothing shall me move.
7 O Lord, thou hast my mountain made
    to stand strong by thy love:

But when that thou, O gracious God,
    didst hide thy face from me,
Then quickly was my prosp'rous state
    turn'd into misery.
8 Wherefore unto the Lord my cry
    I caused to ascend:
My humble supplication
    I to the Lord did send.

9 What profit is there in my blood,
    when I go down to pit?
Shall unto thee the dust give praise?
    thy truth declare shall it?
10 Hear, Lord, have mercy; help me, Lord:
11   Thou turned hast my sadness
To dancing; yea, my sackcloth loos'd,
    and girded me with gladness;

12 That sing thy praise my glory may,
    and never silent be.
O Lord my God, for evermore
    I will give thanks to thee.

Psalm 31

To the chief Musician, A Psalm of David.

1 IN thee, O Lord, I put my trust,
    sham'd let me never be;

According to thy righteousness
 do thou deliver me.
2 Bow down thine ear to me, with speed
  send me deliverance:
To save me, my strong rock be thou,
 and my house of defence.

3 Because thou art my rock, and thee
  I for my fortress take;
Therefore do thou me lead and guide,
 ev'n for thine own name's sake.
4 And sith thou art my strength, therefore
  pull me out of the net,
Which they in subtilty for me
 so privily have set.

5 Into thine hands I do commit
  my sp'rit: for thou art he,
O thou, JEHOVAH, God of truth,
 that hast redeemed me.
6 Those that do lying vanities
  regard, I have abhorr'd:
But as for me, my confidence
 is fixed on the Lord.

7 I'll in thy mercy gladly joy:
  for thou my miseries
Consider'd hast; thou hast my soul
 known in adversities:
8 And thou hast not inclosed me
  within the en'my's hand;
And by thee have my feet been made
 in a large room to stand.

9   O Lord, upon me mercy have,
      for trouble is on me:
    Mine eye, my belly, and my soul,
      with grief consumed be.
10 Because my life with grief is spent,
      my years with sighs and groans:
    My strength doth fail; and for my sin
      consumed are my bones.

11   I was a scorn to all my foes,
      and to my friends a fear;
    And specially reproach'd of those
      that were my neighbours near:
    When they me saw they from me fled.
12   Ev'n so I am forgot,
    As men are out of mind when dead:
      I'm like a broken pot.

13 For slanders I of many heard;
      fear compass'd me, while they
    Against me did consult, and plot
      to take my life away.
14 But as for me, O Lord, my trust
      upon thee I did lay;
    And I to thee, Thou art my God,
      did confidently say.

15 My times are wholly in thine hand:
      do thou deliver me
    From their hands that mine enemies
      and persecutors be.
16 Thy countenance to shine do thou
      upon thy servant make:

Unto me give salvation,
  for thy great mercies' sake.

17 Let me not be asham'd, O Lord,
  for on thee call'd I have:
Let wicked men be sham'd, let them
  be silent in the grave.
18 To silence put the lying lips,
  that grievous things do say,
And hard reports, in pride and scorn,
  on righteous men do lay.

19 How great's the goodness thou for them
  that fear thee keep'st in store,
And wrought'st for them that trust in thee
  the sons of men before!
20 In secret of thy presence thou
  shalt hide them from man's pride:
From strife of tongues thou closely shalt,
  as in a tent, them hide.

21 All praise and thanks be to the Lord;
  for he hath magnify'd
His wondrous love to me within
  a city fortify'd.
22 For from thine eyes cut off I am,
  I in my haste had said;
My voice yet heard'st thou, when to thee
  with cries my moan I made.

23 O love the Lord, all ye his saints;
  because the Lord doth guard
The faithful, and he plenteously
  proud doers doth reward.

24 Be of good courage, and he strength
   unto your heart shall send,
   All ye whose hope and confidence
   doth on the Lord depend.

Psalm 32

A Psalm of David, Maschil.

1   O BLESSED is the man to whom
       is freely pardoned
   All the transgression he hath done,
   whose sin is covered.
2 Bless'd is the man to whom the Lord
   imputeth not his sin,
   And in whose sp'rit there is no guile,
   nor fraud is found therein.

3 When as I did refrain my speech,
   and silent was my tongue,
   My bones then waxed old, because
   I roared all day long.
4 For upon me both day and night
   thine hand did heavy lie,
   So that my moisture turned is
   in summer's drought thereby.

5 I thereupon have unto thee
   my sin acknowledged,
   And likewise mine iniquity
   I have not covered:
   I will confess unto the Lord
   my trespasses, said I;
   And of my sin thou freely didst
   forgive th' iniquity.

6   For this shall ev'ry godly one
       his prayer make to thee;
    In such a time he shall thee seek,
       as found thou mayest be.
    Surely, when floods of waters great
       do swell up to the brim,
    They shall not overwhelm his soul,
       nor once come near to him.

7   Thou art my hiding-place, thou shalt
       from trouble keep me free:
    Thou with songs of deliverance
       about shalt compass me.

8   I will instruct thee, and thee teach
       the way that thou shalt go;
    And, with mine eye upon thee set,
       I will direction show.

9   Then be not like the horse or mule,
       which do not understand;
    Whose mouth, lest they come near to thee,
       a bridle must command.

10 Unto the man that wicked is
       his sorrows shall abound;
    But him that trusteth in the Lord
       mercy shall compass round.

11 Ye righteous, in the Lord be glad,
       in him do ye rejoice:
    All ye that upright are in heart,
       for joy lift up your voice.

Psalm 33

1 YE righteous, in the Lord rejoice;
    it comely is and right,
That upright men, with thankful voice,
    should praise the Lord of might.

2 Praise God with harp, and unto him
    sing with the psaltery;
Upon a ten-string'd instrument
    make ye sweet melody.

3 A new song to him sing, and play
    with loud noise skilfully;

4 For right is God's word, all his works
    are done in verity.

5 To judgment and to righteousness
    a love he beareth still;
The loving-kindness of the Lord
    the earth throughout doth fill.

6 The heavens by the word of God
    did their beginning take;
And by the breathing of his mouth
    he all their hosts did make.

7 The waters of the seas he brings
    together as an heap;
And in storehouses, as it were,
    he layeth up the deep.

8 Let earth, and all that live therein,
    with rev'rence fear the Lord;
Let all the world's inhabitants
    dread him with one accord.

9 For he did speak the word, and done
    it was without delay;

Established it firmly stood,
    whatever he did say.

10 God doth the counsel bring to nought
    which heathen folk do take;
  And what the people do devise
    of none effect doth make.
11 O but the counsel of the Lord
    doth stand for ever sure;
  And of his heart the purposes
    from age to age endure.

12 That nation blessed is, whose God
    JEHOVAH is, and those
  A blessed people are, whom for
    his heritage he chose.
13 The Lord from heav'n sees and beholds
    all sons of men full well:
14 He views all from his dwelling-place
    that in the earth do dwell.

15 He forms their hearts alike, and all
    their doings he observes.
16 Great hosts save not a king, much strength
    no mighty man preserves.
17 An horse for preservation
    is a deceitful thing;
  And by the greatness of his strength
    can no deliv'rance bring.

18 Behold, on those that do him fear
    the Lord doth set his eye;
  Ev'n those who on his mercy do
    with confidence rely.

19 From death to free their soul, in dearth
  life unto them to yield.
20 Our soul doth wait upon the Lord;
  he is our help and shield.

21 Sith in his holy name we trust,
  our heart shall joyful be.
22 Lord, let thy mercy be on us,
  as we do hope in thee.

Psalm 34

*A Psalm of David, when he changed his behaviour before
Abimelech; who drove him away, and he departed.*

1 GOD will I bless all times; his praise
  my mouth shall still express.
2 My soul shall boast in God: the meek
  shall hear with joyfulness.
3 Extol the Lord with me, let us
  exalt his name together.
4 I sought the Lord, he heard, and did
  me from all fears deliver.

5 They look'd to him, and lighten'd were:
  not shamed were their faces.
6 This poor man cry'd, God heard, and sav'd
  him from all his distresses.
7 The angel of the Lord encamps,
  and round encompasseth
All those about that do him fear,
  and them delivereth.

8 O taste and see that God is good:
  who trusts in him is bless'd.

9   Fear God his saints: none that him fear
     shall be with want oppress'd.
10 The lions young may hungry be,
     and they may lack their food:
   But they that truly seek the Lord
     shall not lack any good.

11 O children, hither do ye come,
     and unto me give ear;
   I shall you teach to understand
     how ye the Lord should fear.
12 What man is he that life desires,
     to see good would live long?
13 Thy lips refrain from speaking guile,
     and from ill words thy tongue.

14 Depart from ill, do good, seek peace,
     pursue it earnestly.
15 God's eyes are on the just; his ears
     are open to their cry.
16 The face of God is set against
     those that do wickedly,
   That he may quite out from the earth
     cut off their memory.

17 The righteous cry unto the Lord,
     he unto them gives ear;
   And they out of their troubles all
     by him deliver'd are.
18 The Lord is ever nigh to them
     that be of broken sp'rit;
   To them he safety doth afford
     that are in heart contrite.

19 The troubles that afflict the just
   in number many be;
   But yet at length out of them all
   the Lord doth set him free.
20 He carefully his bones doth keep,
   whatever can befall;
   That not so much as one of them
   can broken be at all.

21 Ill shall the wicked slay; laid waste
   shall be who hate the just.
22 The Lord redeems his servants' souls;
   none perish that him trust.

Psalm 35

A Psalm of David.

1 PLEAD, Lord, with those that plead; and
   fight
   with those that fight with me.
2 Of shield and buckler take thou hold,
   stand up mine help to be.
3 Draw also out the spear, and do
   against them stop the way
   That me pursue: unto my soul,
   I'm thy salvation, say.

4 Let them confounded be and sham'd
   that for my soul have sought:
   Who plot my hurt turn'd back be they,
   and to confusion brought.
5 Let them be like unto the chaff
   that flies before the wind;
   And let the angel of the Lord
   pursue them hard behind.

6 With darkness cover thou their way,
  and let it slipp'ry prove;
And let the angel of the Lord
  pursue them from above.
7 For without cause have they for me
  their net hid in a pit,
They also have without a cause
  for my soul digged it.

8 Let ruin seize him unawares;
  his net he hid withal
Himself let catch; and in the same
  destruction let him fall.
9 My soul in God shall joy; and glad
  in his salvation be:
10 And all my bones shall say, O Lord,
  who is like unto thee,

Which dost the poor set free from him
  that is for him too strong;
The poor and needy from the man
  that spoils and does him wrong?
11 False witnesses rose; to my charge
  things I not knew they laid.
12 They, to the spoiling of my soul,
  me ill for good repaid.

13 But as for me, when they were sick,
  in sackcloth sad I mourn'd:
My humbled soul did fast, my pray'r
  into my bosom turn'd.
14 Myself I did behave as he
  had been my friend or brother;

I heavily bow'd down, as one
    that mourneth for his mother.

15 But in my trouble they rejoic'd,
    gath'ring themselves together;
Yea, abjects vile together did
    themselves against me gather:
I knew it not; they did me tear,
    and quiet would not be.
16 With mocking hypocrites, at feasts
    they gnash'd their teeth at me.

17 How long, Lord, look'st thou on? from those
    destructions they intend
Rescue my soul, from lions young
    my darling do defend.
18 I will give thanks to thee, O Lord,
    within th' assembly great;
And where much people gather'd are
    thy praises forth will set.

19 Let not my wrongful enemies
    proudly rejoice o'er me;
Nor who me hate without a cause,
    let them wink with the eye.
20 For peace they do not speak at all;
    but crafty plots prepare
Against all those within the land
    that meek and quiet are.

21 With mouths set wide, they 'gainst me said,
    Ha, ha! our eye doth see.
22 Lord, thou hast seen, hold not thy peace;
    Lord, be not far from me.

23 Stir up thyself; wake, that thou may'st
    judgment to me afford,
Ev'n to my cause, O thou that art
    my only God and Lord.

24 O Lord my God, do thou me judge
    after thy righteousness;
And let them not their joy 'gainst me
    triumphantly express:
25 Nor let them say within their hearts,
    Ah, we would have it thus;
Nor suffer them to say, that he
    is swallow'd up by us.

26 Sham'd and confounded be they all
    that at my hurt are glad;
Let those against me that do boast
    with shame and scorn be clad.
27 Let them that love my righteous cause
    be glad, shout, and not cease
To say, The Lord be magnify'd,
    who loves his servant's peace.

28 Thy righteousness shall also be
    declared by my tongue;
The praises that belong to thee
    speak shall it all day long.

Psalm 36

To the chief Musician, A Psalm of David the servant of the Lord.

1   THE wicked man's transgression
    within my heart thus says,
Undoubtedly the fear of God
    is not before his eyes.

2 Because himself he flattereth
  in his own blinded eye,
 Until the hatefulness be found
  of his iniquity.

3 Words from his mouth proceeding are,
  fraud and iniquity:
 He to be wise, and to do good,
  hath left off utterly.
4 He mischief, lying on his bed,
  most cunningly doth plot:
 He sets himself in ways not good,
  ill he abhorreth not.

5 Thy mercy, Lord, is in the heav'ns;
  thy truth doth reach the clouds:
6 Thy justice is like mountains great;
  thy judgments deep as floods:
 Lord, thou preservest man and beast.
7 How precious is thy grace!
 Therefore in shadow of thy wings
  men's sons their trust shall place.

8 They with the fatness of thy house
  shall be well satisfy'd;
 From rivers of thy pleasures thou
  wilt drink to them provide.
9 Because of life the fountain pure
  remains alone with thee;
 And in that purest light of thine
  we clearly light shall see.

10 Thy loving-kindness unto them
  continue that thee know;

And still on men upright in heart
   thy righteousness bestow.
11 Let not the foot of cruel pride
   come, and against me stand;
And let me not removed be,
   Lord, by the wicked's hand.

12 There fallen are they, and ruined,
   that work iniquities:
Cast down they are, and never shall
   be able to arise.

Psalm 37

A Psalm of David.

1 FOR evil-doers fret thou not
   thyself unquietly;
Nor do thou envy bear to those
   that work iniquity.
2 For, even like unto the grass,
   soon be cut down shall they;
And, like the green and tender herb,
   they wither shall away.

3 Set thou thy trust upon the Lord,
   and be thou doing good;
And so thou in the land shalt dwell,
   and verily have food.
4 Delight thyself in God; he'll give
   thine heart's desire to thee.
5 Thy way to God commit, him trust,
   it bring to pass shall he.

6 And, like unto the light, he shall
   thy righteousness display;

And he thy judgment shall bring forth
   like noon-tide of the day.
7 Rest in the Lord, and patiently
   wait for him: do not fret
For him who, prosp'ring in his way,
   success in sin doth get.

8 Do thou from anger cease, and wrath
   see thou forsake also:
Fret not thyself in any wise,
   that evil thou should'st do.
9 For those that evil doers are
   shall be cut off and fall:
But those that wait upon the Lord
   the earth inherit shall.

10 For yet a little while, and then
   the wicked shall not be;
His place thou shalt consider well,
   but it thou shalt not see.
11 But by inheritance the earth
   the meek ones shall possess:
They also shall delight themselves
   in an abundant peace.

12 The wicked plots against the just,
   and at him whets his teeth:
13 The Lord shall laugh at him, because
   his day he coming seeth.
14 The wicked have drawn out the sword,
   and bent their bow, to slay
The poor and needy, and to kill
   men of an upright way.

15 But their own sword, which they have
              drawn,
    shall enter their own heart:
  Their bows which they have bent shall
              break,
    and into pieces part.
16 A little that a just man hath
    is more and better far
  Than is the wealth of many such
    as lewd and wicked are.

17 For sinners' arms shall broken be;
    but God the just sustains.
18 God knows the just man's days, and still
    their heritage remains.
19 They shall not be asham'd when they
    the evil time do see;
  And when the days of famine are,
    they satisfy'd shall be.

20 But wicked men, and foes of God,
    as fat of lambs, decay;
  They shall consume, yea, into smoke
    they shall consume away.
21 The wicked borrows, but the same
    again he doth not pay;
  Whereas the righteous mercy shews,
    and gives his own away.

22 For such as blessed be of him
    the earth inherit shall;
  And they that cursed are of him
    shall be destroyed all.

23 A good man's footsteps by the Lord
    are ordered aright;
And in the way wherein he walks
    he greatly doth delight.

24 Although he fall, yet shall he not
    be cast down utterly;
Because the Lord with his own hand
    upholds him mightily.
25 I have been young, and now am old,
    yet have I never seen
The just man left, nor that his seed
    for bread have beggars been.

26 He's ever merciful, and lends:
    his seed is bless'd therefore.
27 Depart from evil, and do good,
    and dwell for evermore.
28 For God loves judgment, and his saints
    leaves not in any case;
They are kept ever: but cut off
    shall be the sinner's race.

29 The just inherit shall the land,
    and ever in it dwell:
30 The just man's mouth doth wisdom speak;
    his tongue doth judgment tell.
31 In's heart the law is of his God,
    his steps slide not away.
32 The wicked man doth watch the just,
    and seeketh him to slay.

33 Yet him the Lord will not forsake,
    nor leave him in his hands:

The righteous will he not condemn,
  when he in judgment stands.
34 Wait on the Lord, and keep his way,
  and thee exalt shall he
Th' earth to inherit; when cut off
  the wicked thou shalt see.

35 I saw the wicked great in pow'r,
  spread like a green bay-tree:
36 He pass'd, yea, was not; him I sought,
  but found he could not be.
37 Mark thou the perfect, and behold
  the man of uprightness;
Because that surely of this man
  the latter end is peace.

38 But those men that transgressors are
  shall be destroy'd together;
The latter end of wicked men
  shall be cut off for ever.
39 But the salvation of the just
  is from the Lord above;
He in the time of their distress
  their stay and strength doth prove.

40 The Lord shall help, and them deliver:
  he shall them free and save
From wicked men; because in him
  their confidence they have.

Psalm 38

A Psalm of David, to bring to remembrance.

1 IN thy great indignation,
  O Lord, rebuke me not;

Nor on me lay thy chast'ning hand,
  in thy displeasure hot.
2 For in me fast thine arrows stick,
  thine hand doth press me sore:
3 And in my flesh there is no health,
  nor soundness any more.

This grief I have, because thy wrath
  is forth against me gone;
And in my bones there is no rest,
  for sin that I have done.
4 Because gone up above mine head
  my great transgressions be;
And, as a weighty burden, they
  too heavy are for me.

5 My wounds do stink, and are corrupt;
  my folly makes it so.
6 I troubled am, and much bow'd down;
  all day I mourning go.
7 For a disease that loathsome is
  so fills my loins with pain,
That in my weak and weary flesh
  no soundness doth remain.

8 So feeble and infirm am I,
  and broken am so sore,
That, through disquiet of my heart,
  I have been made to roar.
9 O Lord, all that I do desire
  is still before thine eye;
And of my heart the secret groans
  not hidden are from thee.

10 My heart doth pant incessantly,
    my strength doth quite decay;
  As for mine eyes, their wonted light
    is from me gone away.
11 My lovers and my friends do stand
    at distance from my sore;
  And those do stand aloof that were
    kinsmen and kind before.

12 Yea, they that seek my life lay snares:
    who seek to do me wrong
  Speak things mischievous, and deceits
    imagine all day long.
13 But, as one deaf, that heareth not,
    I suffer'd all to pass;
  I as a dumb man did become,
    whose mouth not open'd was:

14 As one that hears not, in whose mouth
    are no reproofs at all.
15 For, Lord, I hope in thee; my God,
    thou'lt hear me when I call.
16 For I said, Hear me, lest they should
    rejoice o'er me with pride;
  And o'er me magnify themselves,
    when as my foot doth slide.

17 For I am near to halt, my grief
    is still before mine eye:
18 For I'll declare my sin, and grieve
    for mine iniquity.
19 But yet mine en'mies lively are,
    and strong are they beside;

And they that hate me wrongfully
  are greatly multiply'd.

20 And they for good that render ill,
    as en'mies me withstood;
  Yea, ev'n for this, because that I
    do follow what is good.
21 Forsake me not, O Lord; my God,
    far from me never be.
22 O Lord, thou my salvation art,
    haste to give help to me.

Psalm *39*

To the chief Musician, even to Jeduthun,
A Psalm of David.

1 I SAID, I will look to my ways,
    lest with my tongue I sin:
  In sight of wicked men my mouth
    with bridle I'll keep in.
2 With silence I as dumb became,
    I did myself restrain
  From speaking good; but then the more
    increased was my pain.

3 My heart within me waxed hot;
    and, while I musing was,
  The fire did burn; and from my tongue
    these words I did let pass:
4 Mine end, and measure of my days,
    O Lord, unto me show
  What is the same; that I thereby
    my frailty well may know.

5   Lo, thou my days an handbreadth mad'st;
     mine age is in thine eye
    As nothing: sure each man at best
     is wholly vanity.
6   Sure each man walks in a vain show;
     they vex themselves in vain:
    He heaps up wealth, and doth not know
     to whom it shall pertain.

7   And now, O Lord, what wait I for?
     my hope is fix'd on thee.
8   Free me from all my trespasses,
     the fool's scorn make not me.
9   Dumb was I, op'ning not my mouth,
     because this work was thine.
10 Thy stroke take from me; by the blow
     of thine hand I do pine.

11 When with rebukes thou dost correct
     man for iniquity,
    Thou wastes his beauty like a moth:
     sure each man's vanity.
12 Attend my cry, Lord, at my tears
     and pray'rs not silent be:
    I sojourn as my fathers all,
     and stranger am with thee.

13 O spare thou me, that I my strength
     recover may again,
    Before from hence I do depart,
     and here no more remain.

Psalm 40

To the chief Musician, A Psalm of David.

1 I WAITED for the Lord my God,
    and patiently did bear;
  At length to me he did incline
    my voice and cry to hear.

2 He took me from a fearful pit,
    and from the miry clay,
  And on a rock he set my feet,
    establishing my way.

3 He put a new song in my mouth,
    our God to magnify:
  Many shall see it, and shall fear,
    and on the Lord rely.

4 O blessed is the man whose trust
    upon the Lord relies;
  Respecting not the proud, nor such
    as turn aside to lies.

5 O Lord my God, full many are
    the wonders thou hast done;
  Thy gracious thoughts to us-ward far
    above all thoughts are gone:
  In order none can reckon them
    to thee: if them declare,
  And speak of them I would, they more
    than can be number'd are.

6 No sacrifice nor offering
    didst thou at all desire;
  Mine ears thou bor'd: sin-off'ring thou
    and burnt didst not require:

7   Then to the Lord these were my words,
      I come, behold and see;
    Within the volume of the book
      it written is of me:

8   To do thy will I take delight,
      O thou my God that art;
    Yea, that most holy law of thine
      I have within my heart.

9   Within the congregation great
      I righteousness did preach:
    Lo, thou dost know, O Lord, that I
      refrained not my speech.

10 I never did within my heart
      conceal thy righteousness;
    I thy salvation have declar'd,
      and shown thy faithfulness:
    Thy kindness, which most loving is,
      concealed have not I,
    Nor from the congregation great
      have hid thy verity.

11 Thy tender mercies, Lord, from me
      O do thou not restrain:
    Thy loving-kindness, and thy truth,
      let them me still maintain.

12 For ills past reck'ning compass me,
      and mine iniquities
    Such hold upon me taken have,
      I cannot lift mine eyes:

    They more than hairs are on mine head,
      thence is my heart dismay'd.

13 Be pleased, Lord, to rescue me;
    Lord, hasten to mine aid.
14 Sham'd and confounded be they all
    that seek my soul to kill;
Yea, let them backward driven be,
    and sham'd, that wish me ill.

15 For a reward of this their shame
    confounded let them be,
That in this manner scoffing say,
    Aha, aha! to me.
16 In thee let all be glad, and joy,
    who seeking thee abide;
Who thy salvation love, say still,
    The Lord be magnify'd.

17 I'm poor and needy, yet the Lord
    of me a care doth take:
Thou art my help and saviour,
    my God, no tarrying make.

Psalm 41

To the chief Musician, A Psalm of David.

1 BLESSED is he that wisely doth
    the poor man's case consider;
For when the time of trouble is,
    the Lord will him deliver.
2 God will him keep, yea, save alive;
    on earth he bless'd shall live;
And to his enemies' desire
    thou wilt him not up give.

3 God will give strength when he on bed
    of languishing doth mourn;

And in his sickness sore, O Lord,
    thou all his bed wilt turn.
4 I said, O Lord, do thou extend
    thy mercy unto me;
  O do thou heal my soul; for why?
    I have offended thee.

5 Those that to me are enemies,
    of me do evil say,
  When shall he die, that so his name
    may perish quite away?
6 To see me if he comes, he speaks
    vain words: but then his heart
  Heaps mischief to it, which he tells,
    when forth he doth depart.

7 My haters jointly whispering,
    'gainst me my hurt devise.
8 Mischief, say they, cleaves fast to him;
    he li'th, and shall not rise.
9 Yea, ev'n mine own familiar friend,
    on whom I did rely,
  Who ate my bread, ev'n he his heel
    against me lifted high.

10 But, Lord, be merciful to me,
    and up again me raise,
  That I may justly them requite
    according to their ways.
11 By this I know that certainly
    I favour'd am by thee;
  Because my hateful enemy
    triumphs not over me.

12 But as for me, thou me uphold'st
     in mine integrity;
And me before thy countenance
     thou sett'st continually.
13 The Lord, the God of Israel,
     be bless'd for ever then,
From age to age eternally.
     Amen, yea, and amen.

Psalm 42

To the chief Musician, Maschil, for the sons of Korah.

1 L IKE as the hart for water-brooks
       in thirst doth pant and bray;
So pants my longing soul, O God,
     that come to thee I may.
2 My soul for God, the living God,
     doth thirst: when shall I near
Unto thy countenance approach,
     and in God's sight appear?

3 My tears have unto me been meat,
     both in the night and day,
While unto me continually,
     Where is thy God? they say.
4 My soul is poured out in me,
     when this I think upon;
Because that with the multitude
     I heretofore had gone:

With them into God's house I went
     with voice of joy and praise;
Yea, with the multitude that kept
     the solemn holy days.

5 O why art thou cast down, my soul?
     why in me so dismay'd?
   Trust God, for I shall praise him yet,
     his count'nance is mine aid.

6 My God, my soul's cast down in me;
     thee therefore mind I will
   From Jordan's land, the Hermonites,
     and ev'n from Mizar hill.
7 At the noise of thy water-spouts
     deep unto deep doth call;
   Thy breaking waves pass over me,
     yea, and thy billows all.

8 His loving-kindness yet the Lord
     command will in the day,
   His song's with me by night; to God,
     by whom I live, I'll pray:
9 And I will say to God my rock,
     Why me forgett'st thou so?
   Why, for my foes' oppression,
     thus mourning do I go?

10 'Tis as a sword within my bones,
      when my foes me upbraid;
    Ev'n when by them, Where is thy God?
      'tis daily to me said.
11 O why art thou cast down, my soul?
      why, thus with grief opprest,
    Art thou disquieted in me?
      in God still hope and rest:

    For yet I know I shall him praise,
      who graciously to me

The health is of my countenance,
  yea, mine own God is he.

Psalm 43

1 JUDGE me, O God, and plead my cause
     against th' ungodly nation;
     From the unjust and crafty man,
     O be thou my salvation.
2 For thou the God art of my strength;
     why thrusts thou me thee fro'?
   For th' enemy's oppression
     why do I mourning go?

3 O send thy light forth and thy truth;
     let them be guides to me,
   And bring me to thine holy hill,
     ev'n where thy dwellings be.
4 Then will I to God's altar go,
     to God my chiefest joy:
   Yea, God, my God, thy name to praise
     my harp I will employ.

5 Why art thou then cast down, my soul?
     what should discourage thee?
   And why with vexing thoughts art thou
     disquieted in me?
   Still trust in God; for him to praise
     good cause I yet shall have:
   He of my count'nance is the health,
     my God that doth me save.

Psalm 44

To the chief Musician for the sons of Korah, Maschil.

1 O GOD, we with our ears have heard,
    our fathers have us told,
What works thou in their days hadst done,
    ev'n in the days of old.
2 Thy hand did drive the heathen out,
    and plant them in their place;
Thou didst afflict the nations,
    but them thou didst increase.

3 For neither got their sword the land,
    nor did their arm them save;
But thy right hand, arm, countenance;
    for thou them favour gave.
4 Thou art my King: for Jacob, Lord,
    deliv'rances command.
5 Through thee we shall push down our foes,
    that do against us stand:

We, through thy name, shall tread down
        those
    that ris'n against us have.
6 For in my bow I shall not trust,
    nor shall my sword me save.
7 But from our foes thou hast us sav'd,
    our haters put to shame.
8 In God we all the day do boast,
    and ever praise thy name.

9 But now we are cast off by thee,
    and us thou putt'st to shame;
And when our armies do go forth,
    thou go'st not with the same.

10 Thou mak'st us from the enemy,
    faint-hearted, to turn back;
  And they who hate us for themselves
    our spoils away do take.

11 Like sheep for meat thou gavest us;
    'mong heathen cast we be.
12 Thou didst for nought thy people sell;
    their price enrich'd not thee.
13 Thou mak'st us a reproach to be
    unto our neighbours near;
  Derision and a scorn to them
    that round about us are.

14 A by-word also thou dost us
    among the heathen make;
  The people, in contempt and spite,
    at us their heads do shake.
15 Before me my confusion
    continually abides;
  And of my bashful countenance
    the shame me ever hides:

16 For voice of him that doth reproach,
    and speaketh blasphemy;
  By reason of th' avenging foe,
    and cruel enemy.
17 All this is come on us, yet we
    have not forgotten thee;
  Nor falsely in thy covenant
    behav'd ourselves have we.

18 Back from thy way our heart not turn'd;
    our steps no straying made;

19 Though us thou brak'st in dragons' place,
    and cover'dst with death's shade.
20 If we God's name forgot, or stretch'd
    to a strange god our hands,
21 Shall not God search this out? for he
    heart's secrets understands.

22 Yea, for thy sake we're kill'd all day,
    counted as slaughter-sheep.
23 Rise, Lord, cast us not ever off;
    awake, why dost thou sleep?
24 O wherefore hidest thou thy face?
    forgett'st our cause distress'd,
25 And our oppression? For our soul
    is to the dust down press'd:

Our belly also on the earth
    fast cleaving, hold doth take.
26 Rise for our help, and us redeem,
    ev'n for thy mercies' sake.

Psalm 45

To the chief Musician upon Shoshannim,
for the sons of Korah, Maschil, A Song of loves.

1 MY heart brings forth a goodly thing;
    my words that I indite
Concern the King: my tongue's a pen
    of one that swift doth write.
2 Thou fairer art than sons of men:
    into thy lips is store
Of grace infus'd; God therefore thee
    hath bless'd for evermore.

3 O thou that art the mighty One,
    thy sword gird on thy thigh;

Ev'n with thy glory excellent,
  and with thy majesty.
4 For meekness, truth, and righteousness,
  in state ride prosp'rously;
And thy right hand shall thee instruct
  in things that fearful be.

5 Thine arrows sharply pierce the heart
  of th' en'mies of the King;
And under thy subjection
  the people down do bring.
6 For ever and for ever is,
  O God, thy throne of might;
The sceptre of thy kingdom is
  a sceptre that is right.

7 Thou lovest right, and hatest ill;
  for God, thy God, most high,
Above thy fellows hath with th' oil
  of joy anointed thee.
8 Of aloes, myrrh, and cassia,
  a smell thy garments had,
Out of the iv'ry palaces,
  whereby they made thee glad.

9 Among thy women honourable
  kings' daughters were at hand:
Upon thy right hand did the queen
  in gold of Ophir stand.
10 O daughter, hearken and regard,
  and do thine ear incline;
Likewise forget thy father's house,
  and people that are thine.

11 Then of the King desir'd shall be
    thy beauty veh'mently:
Because he is thy Lord, do thou
    him worship rev'rently.
12 The daughter there of Tyre shall be
    with gifts and off'rings great:
Those of the people that are rich
    thy favour shall entreat.

13 Behold, the daughter of the King
    all glorious is within;
And with embroideries of gold
    her garments wrought have been.
14 She shall be brought unto the King
    in robes with needle wrought;
Her fellow-virgins following
    shall unto thee be brought.

15 They shall be brought with gladness great,
    and mirth on ev'ry side,
Into the palace of the King,
    and there they shall abide.
16 Instead of those thy fathers dear,
    thy children thou may'st take,
And in all places of the earth
    them noble princes make.

17 Thy name remember'd I will make
    through ages all to be:
The people therefore evermore
    shall praises give to thee.

Another of the same

1   **M**Y heart inditing is
      good matter in a song:

I speak the things that I have made,
    which to the King belong:
My tongue shall be as quick,
    his honour to indite,
As is the pen of any scribe
    that useth fast to write.

2 Thou'rt fairest of all men;
    grace in thy lips doth flow:
And therefore blessings evermore
    on thee doth God bestow.
3 Thy sword gird on thy thigh,
    thou that art most of might:
Appear in dreadful majesty,
    and in thy glory bright.

4 For meekness, truth, and right,
    ride prosp'rously in state;
And thy right hand shall teach to thee
    things terrible and great.
5 Thy shafts shall pierce their hearts
    that foes are to the King;
Whereby into subjection
    the people thou shalt bring.

6 Thy royal seat, O Lord,
    for ever shall remain:
The sceptre of thy kingdom doth
    all righteousness maintain.
7 Thou lov'st right, and hat'st ill;
    for God, thy God, most high,
Above thy fellows hath with th' oil
    of joy anointed thee.

8 Of myrrh and spices sweet
    a smell thy garments had,

Out of the iv'ry palaces,
    whereby they made thee glad.
9 And in thy glorious train
    kings' daughters waiting stand;
And thy fair queen, in Ophir gold,
    doth stand at thy right hand.

10 O daughter, take good heed,
    incline, and give good ear;
Thou must forget thy kindred all,
    and father's house most dear.
11 Thy beauty to the King
    shall then delightful be:
And do thou humbly worship him,
    because thy Lord is he.

12 The daughter then of Tyre
    there with a gift shall be,
And all the wealthy of the land
    shall make their suit to thee.
13 The daughter of the King
    all glorious is within;
And with embroideries of gold
    her garments wrought have been.

14 She cometh to the King
    in robes with needle wrought;
The virgins that do follow her
    shall unto thee be brought.
15 They shall be brought with joy,
    and mirth on ev'ry side,
Into the palace of the King,
    and there they shall abide.

16 And in thy fathers' stead,
    thy children thou may'st take,
  And in all places of the earth
    them noble princes make.
17 I will shew forth thy name
    to generations all:
  Therefore the people evermore
    to thee give praises shall.

Psalm 46

To the chief Musician for the sons of Korah,
A Song upon Alamoth.

1 GOD is our refuge and our strength,
    in straits a present aid;
2 Therefore, although the earth remove,
  we will not be afraid:
  Though hills amidst the seas be cast;
3   Though waters roaring make,
  And troubled be; yea though the hills
    by swelling seas do shake.

4 A river is, whose streams do glad
    the city of our God;
  The holy place, wherein the Lord
    most high hath his abode.
5 God in the midst of her doth dwell;
    nothing shall her remove:
  The Lord to her an helper will,
    and that right early, prove.

6 The heathen rag'd tumultuously,
    the kingdoms moved were:
  The Lord God uttered his voice,
    the earth did melt for fear.

7　The Lord of hosts upon our side
　　doth constantly remain:
　The God of Jacob's our refuge,
　　us safely to maintain.

8　Come, and behold what wondrous works
　　have by the Lord been wrought;
　Come, see what desolations
　　he on the earth hath brought.
9　Unto the ends of all the earth
　　wars into peace he turns:
　The bow he breaks, the spear he cuts,
　　in fire the chariot burns.

10　Be still, and know that I am God;
　　among the heathen I
　Will be exalted; I on earth
　　will be exalted high.
11　Our God, who is the Lord of hosts,
　　is still upon our side;
　The God of Jacob our refuge
　　for ever will abide.

Psalm 47

To the chief Musician, A Psalm for the sons of Korah.

1　ALL people, clap your hands; to God
　　with voice of triumph shout:
2　For dreadful is the Lord most high,
　　great King the earth throughout.
3　The heathen people under us
　　he surely shall subdue;
　And he shall make the nations
　　under our feet to bow.

4　The lot of our inheritance
　　chuse out for us shall he,

Of Jacob, whom he loved well,
    ev'n the excellency.
5 God is with shouts gone up, the Lord
    with trumpets sounding high.
6 Sing praise to God, sing praise, sing praise,
    praise to our King sing ye.

7 For God is King of all the earth;
    with knowledge praise express.
8 God rules the nations: God sits on
    his throne of holiness.
9 The princes of the people are
    assembled willingly;
    Ev'n of the God of Abraham
    they who the people be.

For why? the shields that do defend
    the earth are only his:
They to the Lord belong; yea, he
    exalted greatly is.

Psalm 48

A Song and Psalm for the sons of Korah.

1 GREAT is the Lord, and greatly he
    is to be praised still,
Within the city of our God,
    upon his holy hill.
2 Mount Sion stands most beautiful,
    the joy of all the land;
The city of the mighty King
    on her north side doth stand.

3 The Lord within her palaces
    is for a refuge known.

4   For, lo, the kings that gather'd were
      together, by have gone.
5   But when they did behold the same,
      they, wond'ring, would not stay;
    But, being troubled at the sight,
      they thence did haste away.

6   Great terror there took hold on them;
      they were possess'd with fear;
    Their grief came like a woman's pain,
      when she a child doth bear.
7   Thou Tarshish ships with east wind
      break'st:
8   As we have heard it told,
  So, in the city of the Lord,
      our eyes did it behold;

    In our God's city, which his hand
      for ever stablish will.
9   We of thy loving-kindness thought,
      Lord, in thy temple still.
10 O Lord, according to thy name,
      through all the earth's thy praise;
    And thy right hand, O Lord, is full
      of righteousness always.

11 Because thy judgments are made known,
      let Sion mount rejoice;
    Of Judah let the daughters all
      send forth a cheerful voice.
12 Walk about Sion, and go round;
      the high tow'rs thereof tell:
13 Consider ye her palaces,
      and mark her bulwarks well;

That ye may tell posterity.
14   For this God doth abide
Our God for evermore; he will
    ev'n unto death us guide.

Psalm 49

To the chief Musician, A Psalm for the sons of Korah.

1   HEAR this, all people, and give ear,
    all in the world that dwell;
2   Both low and high, both rich and poor.
3   My mouth shall wisdom tell:
My heart shall knowledge meditate.
4   I will incline mine ear
To parables, and on the harp
    my sayings dark declare.

5   Amidst those days that evil be,
    why should I, fearing, doubt?
When of my heels th' iniquity
    shall compass me about.
6   Whoe'er they be that in their wealth
    their confidence do pitch,
And boast themselves, because they are
    become exceeding rich:

7   Yet none of these his brother can
    redeem by any way;
Nor can he unto God for him
    sufficient ransom pay,
8   (Their soul's redemption precious is,
    and it can never be,)
9   That still he should for ever live,
    and not corruption see.

10 For why? he seeth that wise men die,
    and brutish fools also
  Do perish; and their wealth, when dead,
    to others they let go.
11 Their inward thought is, that their house
    and dwelling-places shall
  Stand through all ages; they their lands
    by their own names do call.

12 But yet in honour shall not man
    abide continually;
  But passing hence, may be compar'd
    unto the beasts that die.
13 Thus brutish folly plainly is
    their wisdom and their way;
  Yet their posterity approve
    what they do fondly say.

14 Like sheep they in the grave are laid,
    and death shall them devour;
  And in the morning upright men
    shall over them have pow'r:
  Their beauty from their dwelling shall
    consume within the grave.
15 But from hell's hand God will me free,
    for he shall me receive.

16 Be thou not then afraid when one
    enriched thou dost see,
  Nor when the glory of his house
    advanced is on high:
17 For he shall carry nothing hence
    when death his days doth end;

Nor shall his glory after him
    into the grave descend.

18 Although he his own soul did bless
    whilst he on earth did live;
(And when thou to thyself dost well,
    men will thee praises give;)
19 He to his fathers' race shall go,
    they never shall see light.
20 Man honour'd wanting knowledge is
    like beasts that perish quite.

Psalm 50

A Psalm of Asaph.

1 THE mighty God, the Lord,
    hath spoken, and did call
The earth, from rising of the sun,
    to where he hath his fall.
2 From out of Sion hill,
    which of excellency
And beauty the perfection is,
    God shined gloriously.

3 Our God shall surely come,
    keep silence shall not he:
Before him fire shall waste, great storms
    shall round about him be.
4 Unto the heavens clear
    he from above shall call,
And to the earth likewise, that he
    may judge his people all.

5 Together let my saints
    unto me gather'd be,

Those that by sacrifice have made
  a covenant with me.
6 And then the heavens shall
  his righteousness declare:
Because the Lord himself is he
  by whom men judged are.

7 My people Isr'el hear,
  speak will I from on high,
Against thee I will testify;
  God, ev'n thy God, am I.
8 I for thy sacrifice
  no blame will on thee lay,
Nor for burnt-off'rings, which to me
  thou offer'dst ev'ry day.

9 I'll take no calf nor goats
  from house or fold of thine:
10 For beasts of forests, cattle all
  on thousand hills, are mine.
11 The fowls on mountains high
  are all to me well known;
Wild beasts which in the fields do lie,
  ev'n they are all mine own.

12 Then, if I hungry were,
  I would not tell it thee;
Because the world, and fulness all
  thereof, belongs to me.
13 Will I eat flesh of bulls?
  or goats' blood drink will I?
14 Thanks offer thou to God, and pay
  thy vows to the most High.

15 And call upon me when
    in trouble thou shalt be;
I will deliver thee, and thou
    my name shalt glorify.
16 But to the wicked man
    God saith, My laws and truth
Should'st thou declare? how dar'st thou take
    my cov'nant in thy mouth?

17 Sith thou instruction hat'st,
    which should thy ways direct;
And sith my words behind thy back
    thou cast'st, and dost reject.
18 When thou a thief didst see,
    with him thou didst consent;
And with the vile adulterers
    partaker on thou went.

19 Thou giv'st thy mouth to ill,
    thy tongue deceit doth frame;
20 Thou sitt'st, and 'gainst thy brother
        speak'st,
    thy mother's son dost shame.
21 Because I silence kept,
    while thou these things hast wrought;
That I was altogether like
    thyself, hath been thy thought;

Yet I will thee reprove,
    and set before thine eyes,
In order ranked, thy misdeeds,
    and thine iniquities.
22 Now, ye that God forget,
    this carefully consider;

Lest I in pieces tear you all,
    and none can you deliver.

23 Whoso doth offer praise
    me glorifies; and I
Will shew him God's salvation,
    that orders right his way.

Another of the same

1 THE mighty God, the Lord, hath spoke,
    and call'd the earth upon,
Ev'n from the rising of the sun
    unto his going down.
2 From out of Sion, his own hill,
    where the perfection high
Of beauty is, from thence the Lord
    hath shined gloriously.

3 Our God shall come, and shall no more
    be silent, but speak out:
Before him fire shall waste, great storms
    shall compass him about.
4 He to the heavens from above,
    and to the earth below,
Shall call, that he his judgments may
    before his people show.

5 Let all my saints together be
    unto me gathered;
Those that by sacrifice with me
    a covenant have made.
6 And then the heavens shall declare
    his righteousness abroad:
Because the Lord himself doth come;
    none else is judge but God.

7 Hear, O my people, and I'll speak;
    O Israel by name,
  Against thee I will testify;
    God, ev'n thy God, I am.
8 I for thy sacrifices few
    reprove thee never will,
  Nor for burnt-off'rings to have been
    before me offer'd still.

9 I'll take no bullock nor he-goats
    from house nor folds of thine:
10 For beasts of forests, cattle all
    on thousand hills, are mine.
11 The fowls are all to me well known
    that mountains high do yield;
  And I do challenge as mine own
    the wild beasts of the field.

12 If I were hungry, I would not
    to thee for need complain;
  For earth, and all its fulness, doth
    to me of right pertain.
13 That I to eat the flesh of bulls
    take pleasure dost thou think?
  Or that I need, to quench my thirst,
    the blood of goats to drink?

14 Nay, rather unto me, thy God,
    thanksgiving offer thou:
  To the most High perform thy word,
    and fully pay thy vow:
15 And in the day of trouble great
    see that thou call on me;

I will deliver thee, and thou
my name shalt glorify.

16 But God unto the wicked saith,
Why should'st thou mention make
Of my commands? how dar'st thou in
thy mouth my cov'nant take?
17 Sith it is so that thou dost hate
all good instruction;
And sith thou cast'st behind thy back,
and slight'st my words each one.

18 When thou a thief didst see, then straight
thou join'dst with him in sin,
And with the vile adulterers
thou hast partaker been.
19 Thy mouth to evil thou dost give,
thy tongue deceit doth frame.
20 Thou sitt'st, and 'gainst thy brother speak'st,
thy mother's son to shame.

21 These things thou wickedly hast done,
and I have silent been:
Thou thought'st that I was like thyself,
and did approve thy sin:
But I will sharply thee reprove,
and I will order right
Thy sins and thy transgressions
in presence of thy sight.

22 Consider this, and be afraid,
ye that forget the Lord,
Lest I in pieces tear you all,
when none can help afford.

23 Who off'reth praise me glorifies:
    I will shew God's salvation
To him that ordereth aright
    his life and conversation.

Psalm 51

*To the chief Musician, A Psalm of David, when Nathan the
prophet came unto him, after he had gone in to Bathsheba.*

1 AFTER thy loving-kindness, Lord,
    have mercy upon me:
For thy compassions great, blot out
    all mine iniquity.
2 Me cleanse from sin, and throughly wash
    from mine iniquity:
3 For my transgressions I confess;
    my sin I ever see.

4 'Gainst thee, thee only, have I sinn'd,
    in thy sight done this ill;
That when thou speak'st thou may'st be
              just,
    and clear in judging still.
5 Behold, I in iniquity
    was form'd the womb within;
My mother also me conceiv'd
    in guiltiness and sin.

6 Behold, thou in the inward parts
    with truth delighted art;
And wisdom thou shalt make me know
    within the hidden part.
7 Do thou with hyssop sprinkle me,
    I shall be cleansed so;

Yea, wash thou me, and then I shall
  be whiter than the snow.

8 Of gladness and of joyfulness
    make me to hear the voice;
  That so these very bones which thou
    hast broken may rejoice.
9 All mine iniquities blot out,
    thy face hide from my sin.
10 Create a clean heart, Lord, renew
    a right sp'rit me within.

11 Cast me not from thy sight, nor take
    thy Holy Sp'rit away.
12 Restore me thy salvation's joy;
    with thy free Sp'rit me stay.
13 Then will I teach thy ways unto
    those that transgressors be;
  And those that sinners are shall then
    be turned unto thee.

14 O God, of my salvation God,
    me from blood-guiltiness
  Set free; then shall my tongue aloud
    sing of thy righteousness.
15 My closed lips, O Lord, by thee
    let them be opened;
  Then shall thy praises by my mouth
    abroad be published.

16 For thou desir'st not sacrifice,
    else would I give it thee;
  Nor wilt thou with burnt-offering
    at all delighted be.

17 A broken spirit is to God
   a pleasing sacrifice:
A broken and a contrite heart,
   Lord, thou wilt not despise.

18 Shew kindness, and do good, O Lord,
   to Sion, thine own hill:
The walls of thy Jerusalem
   build up of thy good will.
19 Then righteous off'rings shall thee please,
   and off'rings burnt, which they
With whole burnt-off'rings, and with
         calves,
   shall on thine altar lay.

Psalm 52

*To the chief Musician, Maschil, A Psalm of David, when Doeg the
Edomite came and told Saul, and said unto him, David is come
to the house of Ahimelech.*

1 WHY dost thou boast, O mighty man,
      of mischief and of ill?
The goodness of Almighty God
   endureth ever still.
2 Thy tongue mischievous calumnies
   deviseth subtilely,
Like to a razor sharp to cut,
   working deceitfully.

3 Ill more than good, and more than truth
   thou lovest to speak wrong:
4 Thou lovest all-devouring words,
   O thou deceitful tongue.
5 So God shall thee destroy for aye,
   remove thee, pluck thee out

Quite from thy house, out of the land
of life he shall thee root.

6 The righteous shall it see, and fear,
and laugh at him they shall:
7 Lo, this the man is that did not
make God his strength at all:
But he in his abundant wealth
his confidence did place;
And he took strength unto himself
from his own wickedness.

8 But I am in the house of God
like to an olive green:
My confidence for ever hath
upon God's mercy been.
9 And I for ever will thee praise,
because thou hast done this:
I on thy name will wait; for good
before thy saints it is.

Psalm 53

*To the chief Musician upon Mahalath, Maschil,
A Psalm of David.*

1 THAT there is not a God, the fool
doth in his heart conclude:
They are corrupt, their works are vile,
not one of them doth good.
2 The Lord upon the sons of men
from heav'n did cast his eyes,
To see if any one there was
that sought God, and was wise.

3 They altogether filthy are,
they all are backward gone;

And there is none that doeth good,
    no, not so much as one.
4 These workers of iniquity,
    do they not know at all,
That they my people eat as bread,
    and on God do not call?

5 Ev'n there they were afraid, and stood
    with trembling, all dismay'd,
Whereas there was no cause at all
    why they should be afraid:
For God his bones that thee besieg'd
    hath scatter'd all abroad;
Thou hast confounded them, for they
    despised are of God.

6 Let Isr'el's help from Sion come:
    when back the Lord shall bring
His captives, Jacob shall rejoice,
    and Israel shall sing.

Psalm 54

*To the chief Musician on Neginoth, Maschil, A Psalm of David,
when the Ziphims came and said to Saul, Doth not David hide
himself with us?*

1 SAVE me, O God, by thy great name,
    and judge me by thy strength:
2 My prayer hear, O God; give ear
    unto my words at length.
3 For they that strangers are to me
    do up against me rise;
Oppressors seek my soul, and God
    set not before their eyes.

4　The Lord my God my helper is,
　　lo, therefore I am bold:
　　He taketh part with ev'ry one
　　　that doth my soul uphold.
5　Unto mine enemies he shall
　　mischief and ill repay:
　　O for thy truth's sake cut them off,
　　　and sweep them clean away.

6　I will a sacrifice to thee
　　give with free willingness;
　　Thy name, O Lord, because 'tis good,
　　　with praise I will confess.
7　For he hath me delivered
　　from all adversities;
　　And his desire mine eye hath seen
　　　upon mine enemies.

Psalm 55

To the chief Musician on Neginoth, Maschil,
A Psalm of David.

1　LORD, hear my pray'r, hide not thyself
　　from my entreating voice:
2　Attend and hear me; in my plaint
　　I mourn and make a noise.
3　Because of th' en'my's voice, and for
　　lewd men's oppression great:
　　On me they cast iniquity,
　　　and they in wrath me hate.

4　Sore pain'd within me is my heart:
　　death's terrors on me fall.
5　On me comes trembling, fear and dread
　　o'erwhelmed me withal.

6   O that I, like a dove, had wings,
      said I, then would I flee
  Far hence, that I might find a place
      where I in rest might be.

7   Lo, then far off I wander would,
      and in the desert stay;
8   From windy storm and tempest I
      would haste to 'scape away.
9   O Lord, on them destruction bring,
      and do their tongues divide;
  For in the city violence
      and strife I have espy'd.

10 They day and night upon the walls
      do go about it round:
  There mischief is, and sorrow there
      in midst of it is found.
11 Abundant wickedness there is
      within her inward part;
  And from her streets deceitfulness
      and guile do not depart.

12 He was no foe that me reproach'd,
      then that endure I could;
  Nor hater that did 'gainst me boast,
      from him me hide I would.
13 But thou, man, who mine equal, guide,
      and mine acquaintance wast:
14 We join'd sweet counsels, to God's house
      in company we past.

15 Let death upon them seize, and down
      let them go quick to hell;

For wickedness doth much abound
   among them where they dwell.
16 I'll call on God: God will me save.
17   I'll pray, and make a noise
At ev'ning, morning, and at noon;
   and he shall hear my voice.

18 He hath my soul delivered,
   that it in peace might be
From battle that against me was;
   for many were with me.
19 The Lord shall hear, and them afflict,
   of old who hath abode:
Because they never changes have,
   therefore they fear not God.

20 'Gainst those that were at peace with him
   he hath put forth his hand:
The covenant that he had made,
   by breaking he profan'd.
21 More smooth than butter were his words,
   while in his heart was war;
His speeches were more soft than oil,
   and yet drawn swords they are.

22 Cast thou thy burden on the Lord,
   and he shall thee sustain;
Yea, he shall cause the righteous man
   unmoved to remain.
23 But thou, O Lord my God, those men
   in justice shalt o'erthrow,
And in destruction's dungeon dark
   at last shalt lay them low:

The bloody and deceitful men
   shall not live half their days:
But upon thee with confidence
   I will depend always.

Psalm 56

*To the chief Musician upon Jonath-elem-rechokim, Michtam of
David, when the Philistines took him in Gath.*

1   SHEW mercy, Lord, to me, for man
       would swallow me outright;
   He me oppresseth, while he doth
      against me daily fight.
2   They daily would me swallow up
      that hate me spitefully;
   For they be many that do fight
      against me, O most High.

3   When I'm afraid I'll trust in thee:
4   In God I'll praise his word;
   I will not fear what flesh can do,
      my trust is in the Lord.
5   Each day they wrest my words; their
               thoughts
   'gainst me are all for ill.
6   They meet, they lurk, they mark my steps,
      waiting my soul to kill.

7   But shall they by iniquity
      escape thy judgments so?
   O God, with indignation down
      do thou the people throw.
8   My wand'rings all what they have been
      thou know'st, their number took;

Into thy bottle put my tears:
    are they not in thy book?

9   My foes shall, when I cry, turn back;
    I know't, God is for me.
10 In God his word I'll praise; his word
    in God shall praised be.
11 In God I trust; I will not fear
    what man can do to me.
12 Thy vows upon me are, O God:
    I'll render praise to thee.

13 Wilt thou not, who from death me sav'd,
    my feet from falls keep free,
To walk before God in the light
    of those that living be?

Psalm 57

*To the chief Musician, Al-taschith, Michtam
of David, when he fled from Saul in the cave.*

1   BE merciful to me, O God;
    thy mercy unto me
Do thou extend; because my soul
    doth put her trust in thee:
Yea, in the shadow of thy wings
    my refuge I will place,
Until these sad calamities
    do wholly overpass.

2   My cry I will cause to ascend
    unto the Lord most high;
To God, who doth all things for me
    perform most perfectly.

3 From heav'n he shall send down, and me
  from his reproach defend
 That would devour me: God his truth
  and mercy forth shall send.

4 My soul among fierce lions is,
  I firebrands live among,
 Men's sons, whose teeth are spears and
   darts,
  a sharp sword is their tongue.
5 Be thou exalted very high
  above the heav'ns, O God;
 Let thou thy glory be advanc'd
  o'er all the earth abroad.

6 My soul's bow'd down; for they a net
  have laid, my steps to snare:
 Into the pit which they have digg'd
  for me, they fallen are.
7 My heart is fix'd, my heart is fix'd,
  O God; I'll sing and praise.
8 My glory wake; wake psalt'ry, harp;
  myself I'll early raise.

9 I'll praise thee 'mong the people, Lord;
  'mong nations sing will I:
10 For great to heav'n thy mercy is,
  thy truth is to the sky.
11 O Lord, exalted be thy name
  above the heav'ns to stand:
 Do thou thy glory far advance
  above both sea and land.

Psalm 58

To the chief Musician, Al-taschith, Michtam of David.

1 DO ye, O congregation,
   indeed speak righteousness?
O ye that are the sons of men,
   judge ye with uprightness?
2 Yea, ev'n within your very hearts
   ye wickedness have done;
And ye the vi'lence of your hands
   do weigh the earth upon.

3 The wicked men estranged are,
   ev'n from the very womb;
They, speaking lies, do stray as soon
   as to the world they come.
4 Unto a serpent's poison like
   their poison doth appear;
Yea, they are like the adder deaf,
   that closely stops her ear;

5 That so she may not hear the voice
   of one that charm her would,
No, not though he most cunning were,
   and charm most wisely could.
6 Their teeth, O God, within their mouth
   break thou in pieces small;
The great teeth break thou out, O Lord,
   of these young lions all.

7 Let them like waters melt away,
   which downward still do flow:
In pieces cut his arrows all,
   when he shall bend his bow.

8   Like to a snail that melts away,
      let each of them be gone;
   Like woman's birth untimely, that
      they never see the sun.

9   He shall them take away before
      your pots the thorns can find,
   Both living, and in fury great,
      as with a stormy wind.

10   The righteous, when he vengeance sees,
      he shall be joyful then;
   The righteous one shall wash his feet
      in blood of wicked men.

11   So men shall say, The righteous man
      reward shall never miss:
   And verily upon the earth
      a God to judge there is.

Psalm 59

*To the chief Musician, Al-taschith, Michtam of David;
when Saul sent, and they watched the house to kill him.*

1   MY God, deliver me from those
      that are mine enemies;
   And do thou me defend from those
      that up against me rise.

2   Do thou deliver me from them
      that work iniquity;
   And give me safety from the men
      of bloody cruelty.

3   For, lo, they for my soul lay wait:
      the mighty do combine
   Against me, Lord; not for my fault,
      nor any sin of mine.

4   They run, and, without fault in me,
     themselves do ready make:
  Awake to meet me with thy help;
     and do thou notice take.

5   Awake therefore, Lord God of hosts,
     thou God of Israel,
  To visit heathen all: spare none
     that wickedly rebel.
6   At ev'ning they go to and fro;
     they make great noise and sound,
  Like to a dog, and often walk
     about the city round.

7   Behold, they belch out with their mouth,
     and in their lips are swords:
  For they do say thus, Who is he
     that now doth hear our words?
8   But thou, O Lord, shalt laugh at them,
     and all the heathen mock.
9   While he's in pow'r I'll wait on thee;
     for God is my high rock.

10 He of my mercy that is God
     betimes shall me prevent;
  Upon mine en'mies God shall let
     me see mine heart's content.
11 Them slay not, lest my folk forget;
     but scatter them abroad
  By thy strong pow'r; and bring them down,
     O thou our shield and God.

12 For their mouth's sin, and for the words
     that from their lips do fly,

Let them be taken in their pride;
    because they curse and lie.
13 In wrath consume them, them consume,
    that so they may not be:
And that in Jacob God doth rule
    to th' earth's ends let them see.

14 At ev'ning let thou them return,
    making great noise and sound,
Like to a dog, and often walk
    about the city round.
15 And let them wander up and down,
    in seeking food to eat;
And let them grudge when they shall not
    be satisfy'd with meat.

16 But of thy pow'r I'll sing aloud;
    at morn thy mercy praise:
For thou to me my refuge wast,
    and tow'r, in troublous days.
17 O God, thou art my strength, I will
    sing praises unto thee;
For God is my defence, a God
    of mercy unto me.

Psalm 60

*To the chief Musician upon Shushan-eduth, Michtam of David, to
teach; when he strove with Aram-naharaim, and with Aram-
zobah, when Joab returned, and smote of Edom in the valley of
salt twelve thousand.*

1 O LORD, thou hast rejected us,
    and scatter'd us abroad;
Thou justly hast displeased been;
    return to us, O God.

2 The earth to tremble thou hast made;
     therein didst breaches make:
   Do thou thereof the breaches heal,
     because the land doth shake.

3 Unto thy people thou hard things
     hast shew'd, and on them sent;
   And thou hast caused us to drink
     wine of astonishment.
4 And yet a banner thou hast giv'n
     to them who thee do fear;
   That it by them, because of truth,
     displayed may appear.

5 That thy beloved people may
     deliver'd be from thrall,
   Save with the pow'r of thy right hand,
     and hear me when I call.
6 God in his holiness hath spoke;
     herein I will take pleasure:
   Shechem I will divide, and forth
     will Succoth's valley measure.

7 Gilead I claim as mine by right;
     Manasseh mine shall be;
   Ephraim is of mine head the strength;
     Judah gives laws for me;
8 Moab's my washing-pot; my shoe
     I'll over Edom throw;
   And over Palestina's land
     I will in triumph go.

9 O who is he will bring me to
     the city fortify'd?

O who is he that to the land
    of Edom will me guide?

10 O God, which hadest us cast off,
    this thing wilt thou not do?
    Ev'n thou, O God, which didest not
    forth with our armies go?

11 Help us from trouble; for the help
    is vain which man supplies.

12 Through God we'll do great acts; he shall
    tread down our enemies.

Psalm 61

To the chief Musician upon Neginoth, A Psalm of David.

1 O GOD, give ear unto my cry;
    unto my pray'r attend.

2 From th' utmost corner of the land
    my cry to thee I'll send.
    What time my heart is overwhelm'd,
    and in perplexity,
    Do thou me lead unto the Rock
    that higher is than I.

3 For thou hast for my refuge been
    a shelter by thy pow'r;
    And for defence against my foes
    thou hast been a strong tow'r.

4 Within thy tabernacle I
    for ever will abide;
    And under covert of thy wings
    with confidence me hide.

5 For thou the vows that I did make,
    O Lord my God, didst hear:

Thou hast giv'n me the heritage
    of those thy name that fear.
6 A life prolong'd for many days
    thou to the king shalt give;
Like many generations be
    the years which he shall live.

7 He in God's presence his abode
    for evermore shall have:
O do thou truth and mercy both
    prepare, that may him save.
8 And so will I perpetually
    sing praise unto thy name;
That having made my vows, I may
    each day perform the same.

Psalm 62

To the chief Musician, to Jeduthun, A Psalm of David.

1 MY soul with expectation
    depends on God indeed;
My strength and my salvation doth
    from him alone proceed.
2 He only my salvation is,
    and my strong rock is he:
He only is my sure defence;
    much mov'd I shall not be.

3 How long will ye against a man
    plot mischief? ye shall all
Be slain; ye as a tott'ring fence
    shall be, and bowing wall.
4 They only plot to cast him down
    from his excellency:

They joy in lies; with mouth they bless,
  but they curse inwardly.

5 My soul, wait thou with patience
    upon thy God alone;
  On him dependeth all my hope
    and expectation.
6 He only my salvation is,
    and my strong rock is he;
  He only is my sure defence:
    I shall not moved be.

7 In God my glory placed is,
    and my salvation sure;
  In God the rock is of my strength,
    my refuge most secure.
8 Ye people, place your confidence
    in him continually;
  Before him pour ye out your heart;
    God is our refuge high.

9 Surely mean men are vanity,
    and great men are a lie;
  In balance laid, they wholly are
    more light than vanity.
10 Trust ye not in oppression,
    in robb'ry be not vain;
  On wealth set not your hearts, when as
    increased is your gain.

11 God hath it spoken once to me,
    yea, this I heard again,
  That power to Almighty God
    alone doth appertain.

12 Yea, mercy also unto thee
      belongs, O Lord, alone:
  For thou according to his work
      rewardest ev'ry one.

Psalm 63

A Psalm of David, when he was in the wilderness of Judah.

1 LORD, thee my God, I'll early seek:
      my soul doth thirst for thee;
  My flesh longs in a dry parch'd land,
      wherein no waters be:

2 That I thy power may behold,
      and brightness of thy face,
  As I have seen thee heretofore
      within thy holy place.

3 Since better is thy love than life,
      my lips thee praise shall give.

4 I in thy name will lift my hands,
      and bless thee while I live.

5 Ev'n as with marrow and with fat
      my soul shall filled be;
  Then shall my mouth with joyful lips
      sing praises unto thee:

6 When I do thee upon my bed
      remember with delight,
  And when on thee I meditate
      in watches of the night.

7 In shadow of thy wings I'll joy;
      for thou mine help hast been.

8 My soul thee follows hard; and me
      thy right hand doth sustain.

9 Who seek my soul to spill shall sink
    down to earth's lowest room.
10 They by the sword shall be cut off,
    and foxes' prey become.
11 Yet shall the king in God rejoice,
    and each one glory shall
  That swear by him: but stopp'd shall be
    the mouth of liars all.

Psalm 64

To the chief Musician, A Psalm of David.

1 WHEN I to thee my prayer make,
    Lord, to my voice give ear;
  My life save from the enemy,
    of whom I stand in fear.
2 Me from their secret counsel hide
    who do live wickedly;
  From insurrection of those men
    that work iniquity:

3 Who do their tongues with malice whet,
    and make them cut like swords;
  In whose bent bows are arrows set,
    ev'n sharp and bitter words:
4 That they may at the perfect man
    in secret aim their shot;
  Yea, suddenly they dare at him
    to shoot, and fear it not.

5 In ill encourage they themselves,
    and their snares close do lay:
  Together conference they have;
    Who shall them see? they say.

6　They have search'd out iniquities,
　　　a perfect search they keep:
　　Of each of them the inward thought,
　　　and very heart, is deep.

7　God shall an arrow shoot at them,
　　　and wound them suddenly:
8　So their own tongue shall them confound;
　　　all who them see shall fly.
9　And on all men a fear shall fall,
　　　God's works they shall declare;
　　For they shall wisely notice take
　　　what these his doings are.

10　In God the righteous shall rejoice,
　　　and trust upon his might;
　　Yea, they shall greatly glory all
　　　in heart that are upright.

Psalm 65

To the chief Musician, A Psalm and Song of David.

1　PRAISE waits for thee in Sion, Lord:
　　　to thee vows paid shall be.
2　O thou that hearer art of pray'r,
　　　all flesh shall come to thee.
3　Iniquities, I must confess,
　　　prevail against me do:
　　But as for our transgressions,
　　　them purge away shalt thou.

4　Bless'd is the man whom thou dost chuse,
　　　and mak'st approach to thee,
　　That he within thy courts, O Lord,
　　　may still a dweller be:

We surely shall be satisfy'd
    with thy abundant grace,
And with the goodness of thy house,
    ev'n of thy holy place.

5   O God of our salvation,
    thou, in thy righteousness,
By fearful works unto our pray'rs
    thine answer dost express:
Therefore the ends of all the earth,
    and those afar that be
Upon the sea, their confidence,
    O Lord, will place in thee.

6   Who, being girt with pow'r, sets fast
    by his great strength the hills.
7   Who noise of seas, noise of their waves,
    and people's tumult, stills.
8   Those in the utmost parts that dwell
    are at thy signs afraid:
Th' outgoings of the morn and ev'n
    by thee are joyful made.

9   The earth thou visit'st, wat'ring it;
    thou mak'st it rich to grow
With God's full flood; thou corn prepar'st,
    when thou provid'st it so.
10 Her rigs thou wat'rest plenteously,
    her furrows settelest:
With show'rs thou dost her mollify,
    her spring by thee is blest.

11 So thou the year most lib'rally
    dost with thy goodness crown;

And all thy paths abundantly
    on us drop fatness down.
12 They drop upon the pastures wide,
    that do in deserts lie;
The little hills on ev'ry side
    rejoice right pleasantly.

13 With flocks the pastures clothed be,
    the vales with corn are clad;
And now they shout and sing to thee,
    for thou hast made them glad.

Psalm 66

To the chief Musician, A Song or Psalm.

1 ALL lands to God in joyful sounds,
    aloft your voices raise.
2 Sing forth the honour of his name,
    and glorious make his praise.
3 Say unto God, How terrible
    in all thy works art thou!
Through thy great pow'r thy foes to thee
    shall be constrain'd to bow.

4 All on the earth shall worship thee,
    they shall thy praise proclaim
In songs: they shall sing cheerfully
    unto thy holy name.
5 Come, and the works that God hath wrought
    with admiration see:
In's working to the sons of men
    most terrible is he.

6 Into dry land the sea he turn'd,
    and they a passage had;

Ev'n marching through the flood on foot,
    there we in him were glad.
7 He ruleth ever by his pow'r;
    his eyes the nations see:
    O let not the rebellious ones
    lift up themselves on high.

8 Ye people, bless our God; aloud
    the voice speak of his praise:
9 Our soul in life who safe preserves,
    our foot from sliding stays.
10 For thou didst prove and try us, Lord,
    as men do silver try;
11 Brought'st us into the net, and mad'st
    bands on our loins to lie.

12 Thou hast caus'd men ride o'er our heads;
    and though that we did pass
    Through fire and water, yet thou brought'st
    us to a wealthy place.
13 I'll bring burnt-off'rings to thy house;
    to thee my vows I'll pay,
14 Which my lips utter'd, my mouth spake,
    when trouble on me lay.

15 Burnt-sacrifices of fat rams
    with incense I will bring;
    Of bullocks and of goats I will
    present an offering.
16 All that fear God, come, hear, I'll tell
    what he did for my soul.
17 I with my mouth unto him cry'd,
    my tongue did him extol.

18 If in my heart I sin regard,
  the Lord me will not hear:
19 But surely God me heard, and to
  my prayer's voice gave ear.
20 O let the Lord, our gracious God,
  for ever blessed be,
Who turned not my pray'r from him,
  nor yet his grace from me.

Psalm 67

To the chief Musician on Neginoth, A Psalm or Song.

1 LORD, bless and pity us,
  shine on us with thy face:
2 That th' earth thy way, and nations all
  may know thy saving grace.
3 Let people praise thee, Lord;
  let people all thee praise.
4 O let the nations be glad,
  in songs their voices raise:

Thou'lt justly people judge,
  on earth rule nations all.
5 Let people praise thee, Lord; let them
  praise thee, both great and small.
6 The earth her fruit shall yield,
  our God shall blessing send.
7 God shall us bless; men shall him fear
  unto earth's utmost end.

Another of the same

1 LORD, unto us be merciful,
  do thou us also bless;

And graciously cause shine on us
    the brightness of thy face:
2 That so thy way upon the earth
    to all men may be known;
  Also among the nations all
    thy saving health be shown.

3 O let the people praise thee, Lord;
    let people all thee praise.
4 O let the nations be glad,
    and sing for joy always:
  For rightly thou shalt people judge,
    and nations rule on earth.
5 Let people praise thee, Lord; let all
    the folk praise thee with mirth.

6 Then shall the earth yield her increase;
    God, our God, bless us shall.
7 God shall us bless; and of the earth
    the ends shall fear him all.

Psalm 68

To the chief Musician, A Psalm or Song of David.

1 L ET God arise, and scattered
    let all his en'mies be;
  And let all those that do him hate
    before his presence flee.
2 As smoke is driv'n, so drive thou them;
    as fire melts wax away,
  Before God's face let wicked men
    so perish and decay.

3 But let the righteous be glad:
    let them before God's sight

> Be very joyful; yea, let them
> rejoice with all their might.

4 To God sing, to his name sing praise;
> extol him with your voice,
> That rides on heav'n, by his name JAH,
> before his face rejoice.

5 Because the Lord a father is
> unto the fatherless;
> God is the widow's judge, within
> his place of holiness.

6 God doth the solitary set
> in fam'lies: and from bands
> The chain'd doth free; but rebels do
> inhabit parched lands.

7 O God, what time thou didst go forth
> before thy people's face;
> And when through the great wilderness
> thy glorious marching was;

8 Then at God's presence shook the earth,
> then drops from heaven fell;
> This Sinai shook before the Lord,
> the God of Israel.

9 O God, thou to thine heritage
> didst send a plenteous rain,
> Whereby thou, when it weary was,
> didst it refresh again.

10 Thy congregation then did make
> their habitation there:
> Of thine own goodness for the poor,
> O God, thou didst prepare.

11 The Lord himself did give the word,
    the word abroad did spread;
Great was the company of them
    the same who published.
12 Kings of great armies foiled were,
    and forc'd to flee away;
And women, who remain'd at home,
    did distribute the prey.

13 Though ye have lien among the pots,
    like doves ye shall appear,
Whose wings with silver, and with gold
    whose feathers cover'd are.
14 When there th' Almighty scatter'd kings,
    like Salmon's snow 'twas white.
15 God's hill is like to Bashan hill,
    like Bashan hill for height.

16 Why do ye leap, ye mountains high?
    this is the hill where God
Desires to dwell; yea, God in it
    for aye will make abode.
17 God's chariots twenty thousand are,
    thousands of angels strong;
In's holy place God is, as in
    mount Sinai, them among.

18 Thou hast, O Lord, most glorious,
    ascended up on high;
And in triumph victorious led
    captive captivity:
Thou hast received gifts for men,
    for such as did rebel;

Yea, ev'n for them, that God the Lord
  in midst of them might dwell.

19 Bless'd be the Lord, who is to us
  of our salvation God;
Who daily with his benefits
  us plenteously doth load.
20 He of salvation is the God,
  who is our God most strong;
And unto God the Lord from death
  the issues do belong.

21 But surely God shall wound the head
  of those that are his foes;
The hairy scalp of him that still
  on in his trespass goes.
22 God said, My people I will bring
  again from Bashan hill;
Yea, from the sea's devouring depths
  them bring again I will;

23 That in the blood of enemies
  thy foot imbru'd may be,
And of thy dogs dipp'd in the same
  the tongues thou mayest see.
24 Thy goings they have seen, O God;
  the steps of majesty
Of my God, and my mighty King,
  within the sanctuary.

25 Before went singers, players next
  on instruments took way;
And them among the damsels were
  that did on timbrels play.

26 Within the congregations
    bless God with one accord:
From Isr'el's fountain do ye bless
    and praise the mighty Lord.

27 With their prince, little Benjamin,
    princes and council there
Of Judah were, there Zabulon's
    and Napht'li's princes were.
28 Thy God commands thy strength; make
                                strong
    what thou wrought'st for us, Lord.
29 For thy house at Jerusalem
    kings shall thee gifts afford.

30 The spearmen's host, the multitude
    of bulls, which fiercely look,
Those calves which people have forth sent,
    O Lord our God, rebuke,
Till ev'ry one submit himself,
    and silver pieces bring:
The people that delight in war
    disperse, O God and King.

31 Those that be princes great shall then
    come out of Egypt lands;
And Ethiopia to God
    shall soon stretch out her hands.
32 O all ye kingdoms of the earth,
    sing praises to this King;
For he is Lord that ruleth all,
    unto him praises sing.

33 To him that rides on heav'ns of heav'ns,
    which he of old did found;

Lo, he sends out his voice, a voice
in might that doth abound.
34 Strength unto God do ye ascribe;
for his excellency
Is over Israel, his strength
is in the clouds most high.

35 Thou'rt from thy temple dreadful, Lord;
Isr'el's own God is he,
Who gives his people strength and pow'r:
O let God blessed be.

Psalm 69

To the chief Musician upon Shoshannim, A Psalm of David.

1 SAVE me, O God, because the floods
do so environ me,
That ev'n unto my very soul
come in the waters be.
2 I downward in deep mire do sink,
where standing there is none:
I am into deep waters come,
where floods have o'er me gone.

3 I weary with my crying am,
my throat is also dry'd;
Mine eyes do fail, while for my God
I waiting do abide.
4 Those men that do without a cause
bear hatred unto me,
Than are the hairs upon my head
in number more they be:

They that would me destroy, and are
mine en'mies wrongfully,

Are mighty: so what I took not,
    to render forc'd was I.
5 Lord, thou my folly know'st, my sins
    not cover'd are from thee.
6 Let none that wait on thee be sham'd,
    Lord God of hosts, for me.

O Lord, the God of Israel,
    let none, who search do make,
And seek thee, be at any time
    confounded for my sake.
7 For I have borne reproach for thee,
    my face is hid with shame.
8 To brethren strange, to mother's sons
    an alien I became.

9 Because the zeal did eat me up,
    which to thine house I bear;
And the reproaches cast at thee
    upon me fallen are.
10 My tears and fasts, t' afflict my soul,
    were turned to my shame.
11 When sackcloth I did wear, to them
    a proverb I became.

12 The men that in the gate do sit
    against me evil spake;
They also that vile drunkards were
    of me their song did make.
13 But, in an acceptable time,
    my pray'r, Lord, is to thee:
In truth of thy salvation, Lord,
    and mercy great, hear me.

14 Deliver me out of the mire,
    from sinking do me keep;
Free me from those that do me hate,
    and from the waters deep.
15 Let not the flood on me prevail,
    whose water overflows;
Nor deep me swallow, nor the pit
    her mouth upon me close.

16 Hear me, O Lord, because thy love
    and kindness is most good;
Turn unto me, according to
    thy mercies' multitude.
17 Nor from thy servant hide thy face:
    I'm troubled, soon attend.
18 Draw near my soul, and it redeem;
    me from my foes defend.

19 To thee is my reproach well known,
    my shame, and my disgrace:
Those that mine adversaries be
    are all before thy face.
20 Reproach hath broke my heart; I'm full
    of grief: I look'd for one
To pity me, but none I found;
    comforters found I none.

21 They also bitter gall did give
    unto me for my meat:
They gave me vinegar to drink,
    when as my thirst was great.
22 Before them let their table prove
    a snare; and do thou make

Their welfare and prosperity
    a trap themselves to take.

23 Let thou their eyes so darken'd be,
        that sight may them forsake;
    And let their loins be made by thee
        continually to shake.
24 Thy fury pour thou out on them,
        and indignation;
    And let thy wrathful anger, Lord,
        fast hold take them upon.

25 All waste and desolate let be
        their habitation;
    And in their tabernacles all
        inhabitants be none.
26 Because him they do persecute,
        whom thou didst smite before;
    They talk unto the grief of those
        whom thou hast wounded sore.

27 Add thou iniquity unto
        their former wickedness;
    And do not let them come at all
        into thy righteousness.
28 Out of the book of life let them
        be raz'd and blotted quite;
    Among the just and righteous
        let not their names be writ.

29 But now become exceeding poor
        and sorrowful am I:
    By thy salvation, O my God,
        let me be set on high.

30 The name of God I with a song
    most cheerfully will praise;
And I, in giving thanks to him,
    his name shall highly raise.

31 This to the Lord a sacrifice
    more gracious shall prove
Than bullock, ox, or any beast
    that hath both horn and hoof.
32 When this the humble men shall see,
    it joy to them shall give:
O all ye that do seek the Lord,
    your hearts shall ever live.

33 For God the poor hears, and will not
    his prisoners contemn.
34 Let heav'n, and earth, and seas, him praise,
    and all that move in them.
35 For God will Judah's cities build,
    and he will Sion save,
That they may dwell therein, and it
    in sure possession have.

36 And they that are his servants' seed
    inherit shall the same;
So shall they have their dwelling there
    that love his blessed name.

Psalm 70

*To the chief Musician, A Psalm of David, to bring to
remembrance.*

1 LORD, haste me to deliver;
    with speed, Lord, succour me.
2 Let them that for my soul do seek
    sham'd and confounded be:

Turn'd back be they, and sham'd,
    that in my hurt delight.
3 Turn'd back be they, Ha, ha! that say,
    their shaming to requite.

4 In thee let all be glad,
    and joy that seek for thee:
Let them who thy salvation love
    say still, God praised be.
5 I poor and needy am;
    come, Lord, and make no stay:
My help thou and deliv'rer art;
    O Lord, make no delay.

Another of the same

1 MAKE haste, O God, me to preserve;
    with speed, Lord, succour me.
2 Let them that for my soul do seek
    sham'd and confounded be:
Let them be turned back, and sham'd,
    that in my hurt delight.
3 Turn'd back be they, Ha, ha! that say,
    their shaming to requite.

4 O Lord, in thee let all be glad,
    and joy that seek for thee:
Let them who thy salvation love
    say still, God praised be.
5 But I both poor and needy am;
    come, Lord, and make no stay:
My help thou and deliv'rer art;
    O Lord, make no delay.

Psalm 71

1 O LORD, my hope and confidence
　　is plac'd in thee alone;
　Then let thy servant never be
　　put to confusion.
2 And let me, in thy righteousness,
　　from thee deliv'rance have:
　Cause me escape, incline thine ear
　　unto me, and me save.

3 Be thou my dwelling-rock, to which
　　I ever may resort:
　Thou gav'st commandment me to save,
　　for thou'rt my rock and fort.
4 Free me, my God, from wicked hands,
　　hands cruel and unjust:
5 For thou, O Lord God, art my hope,
　　and from my youth my trust.

6 Thou from the womb didst hold me up;
　　thou art the same that me
　Out of my mother's bowels took;
　　I ever will praise thee.
7 To many I a wonder am;
　　but thou'rt my refuge strong.
8 Fill'd let my mouth be with thy praise
　　and honour all day long.

9 O do not cast me off, when as
　　old age doth overtake me;
　And when my strength decayed is,
　　then do not thou forsake me.
10 For those that are mine enemies
　　against me speak with hate;

And they together counsel take
    that for my soul lay wait.

11 They said, God leaves him; him pursue
    and take: none will him save.
12 Be thou not far from me, my God:
    thy speedy help I crave.
13 Confound, consume them, that unto
    my soul are enemies:
    Cloth'd be they with reproach and shame
    that do my hurt devise.

14 But I with expectation
    will hope continually;
    And yet with praises more and more
    I will thee magnify.
15 Thy justice and salvation
    my mouth abroad shall show,
    Ev'n all the day; for I thereof
    the numbers do not know.

16 And I will constantly go on
    in strength of God the Lord;
    And thine own righteousness, ev'n thine
    alone, I will record.
17 For even from my youth, O God,
    by thee I have been taught;
    And hitherto I have declar'd
    the wonders thou hast wrought.

18 And now, Lord, leave me not, when I
    old and gray-headed grow:
    Till to this age thy strength and pow'r
    to all to come I show.

19 And thy most perfect righteousness,
    O Lord, is very high,
Who hast so great things done: O God,
    who is like unto thee?

20 Thou, Lord, who great adversities,
    and sore, to me didst show,
Shalt quicken, and bring me again
    from depths of earth below.
21 My greatness and my pow'r thou wilt
    increase, and far extend:
On ev'ry side against all grief
    thou wilt me comfort send.

22 Thee, ev'n thy truth, I'll also praise,
    my God, with psaltery:
Thou Holy One of Israel,
    with harp I'll sing to thee.
23 My lips shall much rejoice in thee,
    when I thy praises sound;
My soul, which thou redeemed hast,
    in joy shall much abound.

24 My tongue thy justice shall proclaim,
    continuing all day long;
For they confounded are, and sham'd,
    that seek to do me wrong.

Psalm 72

A Psalm for Solomon.

1   O LORD, thy judgments give the king,
      his son thy righteousness.
2 With right he shall thy people judge,
    thy poor with uprightness.

3   The lofty mountains shall bring forth
    unto the people peace;
    Likewise the little hills the same
      shall do by righteousness.

4   The people's poor ones he shall judge,
    the needy's children save;
    And those shall he in pieces break
      who them oppressed have.
5   They shall thee fear, while sun and moon
    do last, through ages all.
6   Like rain on mown grass he shall drop,
    or show'rs on earth that fall.

7   The just shall flourish in his days,
    and prosper in his reign:
    He shall, while doth the moon endure,
      abundant peace maintain.
8   His large and great dominion shall
    from sea to sea extend:
    It from the river shall reach forth
      unto earth's utmost end.

9   They in the wilderness that dwell
    bow down before him must;
    And they that are his enemies
      shall lick the very dust.
10 The kings of Tarshish, and the isles,
    to him shall presents bring;
    And unto him shall offer gifts
      Sheba's and Seba's king.

11 Yea, all the mighty kings on earth
    before him down shall fall;

And all the nations of the world
  do service to him shall.
12 For he the needy shall preserve,
  when he to him doth call;
The poor also, and him that hath
  no help of man at all.

13 The poor man and the indigent
  in mercy he shall spare;
He shall preserve alive the souls
  of those that needy are.
14 Both from deceit and violence
  their soul he shall set free;
And in his sight right precious
  and dear their blood shall be.

15 Yea, he shall live, and giv'n to him
  shall be of Sheba's gold:
For him still shall they pray, and he
  shall daily be extoll'd.
16 Of corn an handful in the earth
  on tops of mountains high,
With prosp'rous fruit shall shake, like trees
  on Lebanon that be.

The city shall be flourishing,
  her citizens abound
In number shall, like to the grass
  that grows upon the ground.
17 His name for ever shall endure;
  last like the sun it shall:
Men shall be bless'd in him, and bless'd
  all nations shall him call.

18 Now blessed be the Lord our God,
    the God of Israel,
For he alone doth wondrous works,
    in glory that excel.
19 And blessed be his glorious name
    to all eternity:
The whole earth let his glory fill.
    Amen, so let it be.

The prayers of David the son of Jesse are ended.

Psalm 73
A Psalm of Asaph.

1 YET God is good to Israel,
    to each pure-hearted one.
2 But as for me, my steps near slipp'd,
    my feet were almost gone.
3 For I envious was, and grudg'd
    the foolish folk to see,
When I perceiv'd the wicked sort
    enjoy prosperity.

4 For still their strength continueth firm;
    their death of bands is free.
5 They are not toil'd like other men,
    nor plagu'd, as others be.
6 Therefore their pride, like to a chain,
    them compasseth about;
And, as a garment, violence
    doth cover them throughout.

7 Their eyes stand out with fat; they have
    more than their hearts could wish.

8 They are corrupt; their talk of wrong
 both lewd and lofty is.
9 They set their mouth against the heav'ns
 in their blasphemous talk;
 And their reproaching tongue throughout
 the earth at large doth walk.

10 His people oftentimes for this
 look back, and turn about;
 Sith waters of so full a cup
 to these are poured out.
11 And thus they say, How can it be
 that God these things doth know?
 Or, Can there in the Highest be
 knowledge of things below?

12 Behold, these are the wicked ones,
 yet prosper at their will
 In worldly things; they do increase
 in wealth and riches still.
13 I verily have done in vain
 my heart to purify;
 To no effect in innocence
 washed my hands have I.

14 For daily, and all day throughout,
 great plagues I suffer'd have;
 Yea, ev'ry morning I of new
 did chastisement receive.
15 If in this manner foolishly
 to speak I would intend,
 Thy children's generation,
 behold, I should offend.

16 When I this thought to know, it was
   too hard a thing for me;
17 Till to God's sanctuary I went,
   then I their end did see.
18 Assuredly thou didst them set
   a slipp'ry place upon;
   Them suddenly thou castedst down
   into destruction.

19 How in a moment suddenly
   to ruin brought are they!
   With fearful terrors utterly
   they are consum'd away.
20 Ev'n like unto a dream, when one
   from sleeping doth arise;
   So thou, O Lord, when thou awak'st,
   their image shalt despise.

21 Thus grieved was my heart in me,
   and me my reins opprest:
22 So rude was I, and ignorant,
   and in thy sight a beast.
23 Nevertheless continually,
   O Lord, I am with thee:
   Thou dost me hold by my right hand,
   and still upholdest me.

24 Thou, with thy counsel, while I live,
   wilt me conduct and guide;
   And to thy glory afterward
   receive me to abide.
25 Whom have I in the heavens high
   but thee, O Lord, alone?

And in the earth whom I desire
  besides thee there is none.

26 My flesh and heart doth faint and fail,
    but God doth fail me never:
  For of my heart God is the strength
    and portion for ever.
27 For, lo, they that are far from thee
    for ever perish shall;
  Them that a whoring from thee go
    thou hast destroyed all.

28 But surely it is good for me
    that I draw near to God:
  In God I trust, that all thy works
    I may declare abroad.

Psalm 74

Maschil of Asaph.

1 O GOD, why hast thou cast us off?
    is it for evermore?
  Against thy pasture-sheep why doth
    thine anger smoke so sore?
2 O call to thy rememberance
    thy congregation,
  Which thou hast purchased of old;
    still think the same upon:

  The rod of thine inheritance,
    which thou redeemed hast,
  This Sion hill, wherein thou hadst
    thy dwelling in times past.
3 To these long desolations
    thy feet lift, do not tarry;

For all the ills thy foes have done
  within thy sanctuary.

4 Amidst thy congregations
    thine enemies do roar:
  Their ensigns they set up for signs
    of triumph thee before.
5 A man was famous, and was had
    in estimation,
  According as he lifted up
    his axe thick trees upon.

6 But all at once with axes now
    and hammers they go to,
  And down the carved work thereof
    they break, and quite undo.
7 They fired have thy sanctuary,
    and have defil'd the same,
  By casting down unto the ground
    the place where dwelt thy name.

8 Thus said they in their hearts, Let us
    destroy them out of hand:
  They burnt up all the synagogues
    of God within the land.
9 Our signs we do not now behold;
    there is not us among
  A prophet more, nor any one
    that knows the time how long.

10 How long, Lord, shall the enemy
    thus in reproach exclaim?
  And shall the adversary thus
    always blaspheme thy name?

11 Thy hand, ev'n thy right hand of might,
    why dost thou thus draw back?
  O from thy bosom pluck it out
    for our deliv'rance' sake.

12 For certainly God is my King,
    ev'n from the times of old,
  Working in midst of all the earth
    salvation manifold.
13 The sea, by thy great pow'r, to part
    asunder thou didst make;
  And thou the dragons' heads, O Lord,
    within the waters brake.

14 The leviathan's head thou brak'st
    in pieces, and didst give
  Him to be meat unto the folk
    in wilderness that live.
15 Thou clav'st the fountain and the flood,
    which did with streams abound:
  Thou dry'dst the mighty waters up
    unto the very ground.

16 Thine only is the day, O Lord,
    thine also is the night;
  And thou alone prepared hast
    the sun and shining light.
17 By thee the borders of the earth
    were settled ev'ry where:
  The summer and the winter both
    by thee created were.

18 That th' enemy reproached hath,
    O keep it in record;

And that the foolish people have
  blasphem'd thy name, O Lord.
19 Unto the multitude do not
  thy turtle's soul deliver:
The congregation of thy poor
  do not forget for ever.

20 Unto thy cov'nant have respect;
  for earth's dark places be
Full of the habitations
  of horrid cruelty.
21 O let not those that be oppress'd
  return again with shame:
Let those that poor and needy are
  give praise unto thy name.

22 Do thou, O God, arise and plead
  the cause that is thine own:
Remember how thou art reproach'd
  still by the foolish one.
23 Do not forget the voice of those
  that are thine enemies:
Of those the tumult ever grows
  that do against thee rise.

Psalm 75

To the chief Musician, Al-taschith, A Psalm or Song of Asaph.

1 TO thee, O God, do we give thanks,
  we do give thanks to thee;
Because thy wondrous works declare
  thy great name near to be.
2 I purpose, when I shall receive
  the congregation,

That I shall judgment uprightly
   render to ev'ry one.

3   Dissolved is the land, with all
     that in the same do dwell;
But I the pillars thereof do
     bear up, and stablish well.
4   I to the foolish people said,
     Do not deal foolishly;
And unto those that wicked are,
     Lift not your horn on high.

5   Lift not your horn on high, nor speak
6   with stubborn neck. But know,
That not from east, nor west, nor south,
     promotion doth flow.
7   But God is judge; he puts down one,
     and sets another up.
8   For in the hand of God most high
     of red wine is a cup:

'Tis full of mixture, he pours forth,
     and makes the wicked all
Wring out the bitter dregs thereof;
     yea, and they drink them shall.
9   But I for ever will declare,
     I Jacob's God will praise.
10 All horns of lewd men I'll cut off;
     but just men's horns will raise.

Psalm 76

To the chief Musician on Neginoth, A Psalm or Song of Asaph.

1 IN Judah's land God is well known,
    his name's in Isr'el great:

2   In Salem is his tabernacle,
    in Sion is his seat.
3   There arrows of the bow he brake,
    the shield, the sword, the war.
4   More glorious thou than hills of prey,
    more excellent art far.

5   Those that were stout of heart are spoil'd,
    they slept their sleep outright;
And none of those their hands did find,
    that were the men of might.
6   When thy rebuke, O Jacob's God,
    had forth against them past,
Their horses and their chariots both
    were in a dead sleep cast.

7   Thou, Lord, ev'n thou art he that should
    be fear'd; and who is he
That may stand up before thy sight,
    if once thou angry be?
8   From heav'n thou judgment caus'd be heard;
    the earth was still with fear,
9   When God to judgment rose, to save
    all meek on earth that were.

10 Surely the very wrath of man
    unto thy praise redounds:
Thou to the remnant of his wrath
    wilt set restraining bounds.
11 Vow to the Lord your God, and pay:
    all ye that near him be,
Bring gifts and presents unto him;
    for to be fear'd is he.

12 By him the sp'rits shall be cut off
    of those that princes are:
Unto the kings that are on earth
    he fearful doth appear.

Psalm 77

To the chief Musician, to Jeduthun, A Psalm of Asaph.

1 UNTO the Lord I with my voice,
    I unto God did cry;
Ev'n with my voice, and unto me
    his ear he did apply.
2 I in my trouble sought the Lord,
    my sore by night did run,
And ceased not; my grieved soul
    did consolation shun.

3 I to remembrance God did call,
    yet trouble did remain;
And overwhelm'd my spirit was,
    whilst I did sore complain.
4 Mine eyes, debarr'd from rest and sleep,
    thou makest still to wake;
My trouble is so great that I
    unable am to speak.

5 The days of old to mind I call'd,
    and oft did think upon
The times and ages that are past
    full many years agone.
6 By night my song I call to mind,
    and commune with my heart;
My sp'rit did carefully enquire
    how I might ease my smart.

7 For ever will the Lord cast off,
   and gracious be no more?
8 For ever is his mercy gone?
   fails his word evermore?
9 Is't true that to be gracious
   the Lord forgotten hath?
   And that his tender mercies he
   hath shut up in his wrath?

10 Then did I say, That surely this
   is mine infirmity:
   I'll mind the years of the right hand
   of him that is most High.
11 Yea, I remember will the works
   performed by the Lord:
   The wonders done of old by thee
   I surely will record.

12 I also will of all thy works
   my meditation make;
   And of thy doings to discourse
   great pleasure I will take.
13 O God, thy way most holy is
   within thy sanctuary;
   And what God is so great in pow'r
   as is our God most high?

14 Thou art the God that wonders dost
   by thy right hand most strong:
   Thy mighty pow'r thou hast declar'd
   the nations among.
15 To thine own people with thine arm
   thou didst redemption bring;

To Jacob's sons, and to the tribes
  of Joseph that do spring.

16 The waters, Lord, perceived thee,
  the waters saw thee well;
And they for fear aside did flee;
  the depths on trembling fell.
17 The clouds in water forth were pour'd,
  sound loudly did the sky;
And swiftly through the world abroad
  thine arrows fierce did fly.

18 Thy thunder's voice alongst the heav'n
  a mighty noise did make;
By lightnings lighten'd was the world,
  th' earth tremble did and shake.
19 Thy way is in the sea, and in
  the waters great thy path;
Yet are thy footsteps hid, O Lord;
  none knowledge thereof hath.

20 Thy people thou didst safely lead,
  like to a flock of sheep;
By Moses' hand and Aaron's thou
  didst them conduct and keep.

Psalm 78

Maschil of Asaph.

1 ATTEND, my people, to my law;
  thereto give thou an ear;
The words that from my mouth proceed
  attentively do hear.
2 My mouth shall speak a parable,
  and sayings dark of old;

3 The same which we have heard and known,
   and us our fathers told.

4 We also will them not conceal
   from their posterity;
   Them to the generation
   to come declare will we:
   The praises of the Lord our God,
   and his almighty strength,
   The wondrous works that he hath done,
   we will shew forth at length.

5 His testimony and his law
   in Isr'el he did place,
   And charg'd our fathers it to show
   to their succeeding race;
6 That so the race which was to come
   might well them learn and know;
   And sons unborn, who should arise,
   might to their sons them show:

7 That they might set their hope in God,
   and suffer not to fall
   His mighty works out of their mind,
   but keep his precepts all:
8 And might not, like their fathers, be
   a stiff rebellious race;
   A race not right in heart; with God
   whose sp'rit not stedfast was.

9 The sons of Ephraim, who nor bows
   nor other arms did lack,
   When as the day of battle was,
   they faintly turned back.

10 They brake God's cov'nant, and refus'd
    in his commands to go;
11 His works and wonders they forgot,
    which he to them did show.

12 Things marvellous he brought to pass;
    their fathers them beheld
Within the land of Egypt done,
    yea, ev'n in Zoan's field.
13 By him divided was the sea,
    he caus'd them through to pass;
And made the waters so to stand,
    as like an heap it was.

14 With cloud by day, with light of fire
    all night, he did them guide.
15 In desert rocks he clave, and drink,
    as from great depths, supply'd.
16 He from the rock brought streams, like floods
    made waters to run down.
17 Yet sinning more, in desert they
    provok'd the highest One.

18 For in their heart they tempted God,
    and, speaking with mistrust,
They greedily did meat require
    to satisfy their lust.
19 Against the Lord himself they spake,
    and, murmuring, said thus,
A table in the wilderness
    can God prepare for us?

20 Behold, he smote the rock, and thence
    came streams and waters great;

But can he give his people bread?
    and send them flesh to eat?
21 The Lord did hear, and waxed wroth;
    so kindled was a flame
'Gainst Jacob, and 'gainst Israel
    up indignation came.

22 For they believ'd not God, nor trust
    in his salvation had;
23 Though clouds above he did command,
    and heav'n's doors open made,
24 And manna rain'd on them, and gave
    them corn of heav'n to eat.
25 Man angels' food did eat; to them
    he to the full sent meat.

26 And in the heaven he did cause
    an eastern wind to blow;
And by his power he let out
    the southern wind to go.
27 Then flesh as thick as dust he made
    to rain down them among;
And feather'd fowls, like as the sand
    which li'th the shore along.

28 At his command amidst their camp
    these show'rs of flesh down fell,
All round about the tabernacles
    and tents where they did dwell.
29 So they did eat abundantly,
    and had of meat their fill;
For he did give to them what was
    their own desire and will.

30 They from their lust had not estrang'd
    their heart and their desire;
  But while the meat was in their mouths,
    which they did so require,
31 God's wrath upon them came, and slew
    the fattest of them all;
  So that the choice of Israel,
    o'erthrown by death, did fall.

32 Yet, notwithstanding of all this,
    they sinned still the more;
  And though he had great wonders wrought,
    believ'd him not therefore:
33 Wherefore their days in vanity
    he did consume and waste;
  And by his wrath their wretched years
    away in trouble past.

34 But when he slew them, then they did
    to seek him shew desire;
  Yea, they return'd, and after God
    right early did enquire.
35 And that the Lord had been their Rock,
    they did remember then;
  Ev'n that the high almighty God
    had their Redeemer been.

36 Yet with their mouth they flatter'd him,
    and spake but feignedly;
  And they unto the God of truth
    with their false tongues did lie.
37 For though their words were good, their
        heart
    with him was not sincere;

Unstedfast and perfidious
    they in his cov'nant were.

38 But, full of pity, he forgave
    their sin, them did not slay;
  Nor stirr'd up all his wrath, but oft
    his anger turn'd away.
39 For that they were but fading flesh
    to mind he did recall;
  A wind that passeth soon away,
    and not returns at all.

40 How often did they him provoke
    within the wilderness!
  And in the desert did him grieve
    with their rebelliousness!
41 Yea, turning back, they tempted God,
    and limits set upon
  Him, who in midst of Isr'el is
    the only Holy One.

42 They did not call to mind his pow'r,
    nor yet the day when he
  Deliver'd them out of the hand
    of their fierce enemy;
43 Nor how great signs in Egypt land
    he openly had wrought;
  What miracles in Zoan's field
    his hand to pass had brought.

44 How lakes and rivers ev'ry where
    he turned into blood;
  So that nor man nor beast could drink
    of standing lake or flood.

45 He brought among them swarms of flies,
    which did them sore annoy;
  And divers kinds of filthy frogs
    he sent them to destroy.

46 He to the caterpillar gave
    the fruits of all their soil;
  Their labours he deliver'd up
    unto the locusts' spoil.

47 Their vines with hail, their sycamores
    he with the frost did blast:

48 Their beasts to hail he gave; their flocks
    hot thunderbolts did waste.

49 Fierce burning wrath he on them cast,
    and indignation strong,
  And troubles sore, by sending forth
    ill angels them among.

50 He to his wrath made way; their soul
    from death he did not save;
  But over to the pestilence
    the lives of them he gave.

51 In Egypt land the first-born all
    he smote down ev'ry where;
  Among the tents of Ham, ev'n these
    chief of their strength that were.

52 But his own people, like to sheep,
    thence to go forth he made;
  And he, amidst the wilderness,
    them, as a flock, did lead.

53 And he them safely on did lead,
    so that they did not fear;

Whereas their en'mies by the sea
  quite overwhelmed were.
54 To borders of his sanctuary
  the Lord his people led,
Ev'n to the mount which his right hand
  for them had purchased.

55 The nations of Canaan,
  by his almighty hand,
Before their face he did expel
  out of their native land;
Which for inheritance to them
  by line he did divide,
And made the tribes of Israel
  within their tents abide.

56 Yet God most high they did provoke,
  and tempted ever still;
And to observe his testimonies
  did not incline their will:
57 But, like their fathers, turned back,
  and dealt unfaithfully:
Aside they turned, like a bow
  that shoots deceitfully.

58 For they to anger did provoke
  him with their places high;
And with their graven images
  mov'd him to jealousy.
59 When God heard this, he waxed wroth,
  and much loath'd Isr'el then:
60 So Shiloh's tent he left, the tent
  which he had plac'd with men.

61 And he his strength delivered
     into captivity;
   He left his glory in the hand
     of his proud enemy.
62 His people also he gave o'er
     unto the sword's fierce rage:
   So sore his wrath inflamed was
     against his heritage.

63 The fire consum'd their choice young men;
     their maids no marriage had;
64 And when their priests fell by the sword,
     their wives no mourning made.
65 But then the Lord arose, as one
     that doth from sleep awake;
   And like a giant that, by wine
     refresh'd, a shout doth make:

66 Upon his en'mies' hinder parts
     he made his stroke to fall;
   And so upon them he did put
     a shame perpetual.
67 Moreover, he the tabernacle
     of Joseph did refuse;
   The mighty tribe of Ephraim
     he would in no wise chuse:

68 But he did chuse Jehudah's tribe
     to be the rest above;
   And of mount Sion he made choice,
     which he so much did love.
69 And he his sanctuary built
     like to a palace high,

Like to the earth which he did found
    to perpetuity.

70 Of David, that his servant was,
    he also choice did make,
And even from the folds of sheep
    was pleased him to take:
71 From waiting on the ewes with young,
    he brought him forth to feed
Israel, his inheritance,
    his people, Jacob's seed.

72 So after the integrity
    he of his heart them fed;
And by the good skill of his hands
    them wisely governed.

Psalm *79*

A Psalm of Asaph.

1 O GOD, the heathen enter'd have
    thine heritage; by them
Defiled is thy house: on heaps
    they laid Jerusalem.
2 The bodies of thy servants they
    have cast forth to be meat
To rav'nous fowls; thy dear saints' flesh
    they gave to beasts to eat.

3 Their blood about Jerusalem
    like water they have shed;
And there was none to bury them
    when they were slain and dead.
4 Unto our neighbours a reproach
    most base become are we;

A scorn and laughingstock to them
   that round about us be.

5 How long, Lord, shall thine anger last?
   wilt thou still keep the same?
And shall thy fervent jealousy
   burn like unto a flame?
6 On heathen pour thy fury forth,
   that have thee never known,
And on those kingdoms which thy name
   have never call'd upon.

7 For these are they who Jacob have
   devoured cruelly;
And they his habitation
   have caused waste to lie.
8 Against us mind not former sins;
   thy tender mercies show;
Let them prevent us speedily,
   for we're brought very low.

9 For thy name's glory help us, Lord,
   who hast our Saviour been:
Deliver us; for thy name's sake,
   O purge away our sin.
10 Why say the heathen, Where's their God?
   let him to them be known;
When those who shed thy servants' blood
   are in our sight o'erthrown.

11 O let the pris'ner's sighs ascend
   before thy sight on high;
Preserve those in thy mighty pow'r
   that are design'd to die.

12 And to our neighbours' bosom cause
    it sev'nfold render'd be,
Ev'n the reproach wherewith they have,
    O Lord, reproached thee.

13 So we thy folk, and pasture-sheep,
    shall give thee thanks always;
And unto generations all
    we will shew forth thy praise.

Psalm 80

*To the chief Musician upon Shoshannim-Eduth, A Psalm of
Asaph.*

1 HEAR, Isr'el's Shepherd! like a flock
    thou that dost Joseph guide;
Shine forth, O thou that dost between
    the cherubims abide.
2 In Ephraim's, and Benjamin's,
    and in Manasseh's sight,
O come for our salvation;
    stir up thy strength and might.

3 Turn us again, O Lord our God,
    and upon us vouchsafe
To make thy countenance to shine,
    and so we shall be safe.
4 O Lord of hosts, almighty God,
    how long shall kindled be
Thy wrath against the prayer made
    by thine own folk to thee?

5 Thou tears of sorrow giv'st to them
    instead of bread to eat;
Yea, tears instead of drink thou giv'st
    to them in measure great.

6   Thou makest us a strife unto
     our neighbours round about;
   Our enemies among themselves
     at us do laugh and flout.

7   Turn us again, O God of hosts,
     and upon us vouchsafe
   To make thy countenance to shine,
     and so we shall be safe.

8   A vine from Egypt brought thou hast,
     by thine outstretched hand;
   And thou the heathen out didst cast,
     to plant it in their land.

9   Before it thou a room didst make,
     where it might grow and stand;
   Thou causedst it deep root to take,
     and it did fill the land.

10 The mountains vail'd were with its shade,
     as with a covering;
   Like goodly cedars were the boughs
     which out from it did spring.

11 Upon the one hand to the sea
     her boughs she did out send;
   On th' other side unto the flood
     her branches did extend.

12 Why hast thou then thus broken down,
     and ta'en her hedge away?
   So that all passengers do pluck,
     and make of her a prey.

13 The boar who from the forest comes
     doth waste it at his pleasure;

The wild beast of the field also
    devours it out of measure.

14 O God of hosts, we thee beseech,
    return now unto thine;
Look down from heav'n in love, behold,
    and visit this thy vine:

15 This vineyard, which thine own right hand
    hath planted us among;
And that same branch, which for thyself
    thou hast made to be strong.
16 Burnt up it is with flaming fire,
    it also is cut down:
They utterly are perished,
    when as thy face doth frown.

17 O let thy hand be still upon
    the Man of thy right hand,
The Son of man, whom for thyself
    thou madest strong to stand.
18 So henceforth we will not go back,
    nor turn from thee at all:
O do thou quicken us, and we
    upon thy name will call.

19 Turn us again, Lord God of hosts,
    and upon us vouchsafe
To make thy countenance to shine,
    and so we shall be safe.

Psalm 81

To the chief Musician upon Gittith, A Psalm of Asaph.

1 SING loud to God our strength; with joy
    to Jacob's God do sing.

2 Take up a psalm, the pleasant harp,
     timbrel and psalt'ry bring.
3 Blow trumpets at new-moon, what day
     our feast appointed is:
4 For charge to Isr'el, and a law
     of Jacob's God was this.

5 To Joseph this a testimony
     he made, when Egypt land
   He travell'd through, where speech I heard
     I did not understand.
6 His shoulder I from burdens took,
     his hands from pots did free.
7 Thou didst in trouble on me call,
     and I deliver'd thee:

   In secret place of thundering
     I did thee answer make;
   And at the streams of Meribah
     of thee a proof did take.
8 O thou, my people, give an ear,
     I'll testify to thee;
   To thee, O Isr'el, if thou wilt
     but hearken unto me.

9 In midst of thee there shall not be
     any strange god at all;
   Nor unto any god unknown
     thou bowing down shalt fall.
10 I am the Lord thy God, which did
     from Egypt land thee guide;
   I'll fill thy mouth abundantly,
     do thou it open wide.

11 But yet my people to my voice
    would not attentive be;
And ev'n my chosen Israel
    he would have none of me.
12 So to the lust of their own hearts
    I them delivered;
And then in counsels of their own
    they vainly wandered.

13 O that my people had me heard,
    Isr'el my ways had chose!
14 I had their en'mies soon subdu'd,
    my hand turn'd on their foes.
15 The haters of the Lord to him
    submission should have feign'd;
But as for them, their time should have
    for evermore remain'd.

16 He should have also fed them with
    the finest of the wheat;
Of honey from the rock thy fill
    I should have made thee eat.

Psalm 82

A Psalm of Asaph.

1 IN gods' assembly God doth stand;
    he judgeth gods among.
2 How long, accepting persons vile,
    will ye give judgment wrong?
3 Defend the poor and fatherless;
    to poor oppress'd do right.
4 The poor and needy ones set free;
    rid them from ill men's might.

5 They know not, nor will understand;
    in darkness they walk on:
  All the foundations of the earth
    out of their course are gone.
6 I said that ye are gods, and are
    sons of the Highest all:
7 But ye shall die like men, and as
    one of the princes fall.

8 O God, do thou raise up thyself,
    the earth to judgment call:
  For thou, as thine inheritance,
    shalt take the nations all.

Psalm 83

A Song or Psalm of Asaph.

1 KEEP not, O God, we thee entreat,
    O keep not silence now:
  Do thou not hold thy peace, O God,
    and still no more be thou.
2 For, lo, thine enemies a noise
    tumultuously have made;
  And they that haters are of thee
    have lifted up the head.

3 Against thy chosen people they
    do crafty counsel take;
  And they against thy hidden ones
    do consultations make.
4 Come, let us cut them off, said they,
    from being a nation,
  That of the name of Isr'el may
    no more be mention.

5   For with joint heart they plot, in league
       against thee they combine.
6   The tents of Edom, Ishm'elites,
       Moab's and Hagar's line;
7   Gebal, and Ammon, Amalek,
       Philistines, those of Tyre;
8   And Assur join'd with them, to help
       Lot's children they conspire.

9   Do to them as to Midian,
       Jabin at Kison strand;
10 And Sis'ra, which at En-dor fell,
       as dung to fat the land.
11 Like Oreb and like Zeeb make
       their noble men to fall;
     Like Zeba and Zalmunna like,
       make thou their princes all;

12 Who said, For our possession
       let us God's houses take.
13 My God, them like a wheel, as chaff
       before the wind, them make.
14 As fire consumes the wood, as flame
       doth mountains set on fire,
15 Chase and affright them with the storm
       and tempest of thine ire.

16 Their faces fill with shame, O Lord,
       that they may seek thy name.
17 Let them confounded be, and vex'd,
       and perish in their shame:
18 That men may know that thou, to whom
       alone doth appertain
     The name JEHOVAH, dost most high
       o'er all the earth remain.

Psalm 84

To the chief Musician upon Gittith, A Psalm for the sons of Korah.

1 HOW lovely is thy dwelling-place,
    O Lord of hosts, to me!
The tabernacles of thy grace
    how pleasant, Lord, they be!
2 My thirsty soul longs veh'mently,
    yea faints, thy courts to see:
My very heart and flesh cry out,
    O living God, for thee.

3 Behold, the sparrow findeth out
    an house wherein to rest;
The swallow also for herself
    hath purchased a nest;
Ev'n thine own altars, where she safe
    her young ones forth may bring,
O thou almighty Lord of hosts,
    who art my God and King.

4 Bless'd are they in thy house that dwell,
    they ever give thee praise.
5 Bless'd is the man whose strength thou art,
    in whose heart are thy ways:
6 Who passing thorough Baca's vale,
    therein do dig up wells;
Also the rain that falleth down
    the pools with water fills.

7 So they from strength unwearied go
    still forward unto strength,
Until in Zion they appear
    before the Lord at length.

8 Lord God of hosts, my prayer hear;
   O Jacob's God, give ear.
9 See God our shield, look on the face
   of thine anointed dear.

10 For in thy courts one day excels
    a thousand; rather in
My God's house will I keep a door,
    than dwell in tents of sin.
11 For God the Lord's a sun and shield:
    he'll grace and glory give;
And will withhold no good from them
    that uprightly do live.

12 O thou that art the Lord of hosts,
    that man is truly blest,
Who by assured confidence
    on thee alone doth rest.

Psalm 85

To the chief Musician, A Psalm for the sons of Korah.

1 O LORD, thou hast been favourable
   to thy beloved land:
Jacob's captivity thou hast
   recall'd with mighty hand.
2 Thou pardoned thy people hast
   all their iniquities;
Thou all their trespasses and sins
   hast cover'd from thine eyes.

3 Thou took'st off all thine ire, and turn'dst
   from thy wrath's furiousness.
4 Turn us, God of our health, and cause
   thy wrath 'gainst us to cease.

5 Shall thy displeasure thus endure
    against us without end?
  Wilt thou to generations all
    thine anger forth extend?

6 That in thee may thy people joy,
    wilt thou not us revive?
7 Shew us thy mercy, Lord, to us
    do thy salvation give.
8 I'll hear what God the Lord will speak:
    to his folk he'll speak peace,
  And to his saints; but let them not
    return to foolishness.

9 To them that fear him surely near
    is his salvation;
  That glory in our land may have
    her habitation.
10 Truth met with mercy, righteousness
    and peace kiss'd mutually:
11 Truth springs from earth, and righteousness
    looks down from heaven high.

12 Yea, what is good the Lord shall give;
    our land shall yield increase:
13 Justice, to set us in his steps,
    shall go before his face.

Psalm 86

A Prayer of David.

1 O LORD, do thou bow down thine ear,
    and hear me graciously;
  Because I sore afflicted am,
    and am in poverty.

2   Because I'm holy, let my soul
        by thee preserved be:
     O thou my God, thy servant save,
        that puts his trust in thee.

3   Sith unto thee I daily cry,
        be merciful to me.
4   Rejoice thy servant's soul; for, Lord,
        I lift my soul to thee.
5   For thou art gracious, O Lord,
        and ready to forgive;
     And rich in mercy, all that call
        upon thee to relieve.

6   Hear, Lord, my pray'r; unto the voice
        of my request attend:
7   In troublous times I'll call on thee;
        for thou wilt answer send.
8   Lord, there is none among the gods
        that may with thee compare;
     And like the works which thou hast done,
        not any work is there.

9   All nations whom thou mad'st shall come
        and worship rev'rently
     Before thy face; and they, O Lord,
        thy name shall glorify.
10   Because thou art exceeding great,
        and works by thee are done
     Which are to be admir'd; and thou
        art God thyself alone.

11   Teach me thy way, and in thy truth,
        O Lord, then walk will I;

Unite my heart, that I thy name
  may fear continually.
12 O Lord my God, with all my heart
  to thee I will give praise;
And I the glory will ascribe
  unto thy name always:

13 Because thy mercy toward me
  in greatness doth excel;
And thou deliver'd hast my soul
  out from the lowest hell.
14 O God, the proud against me rise,
  and vi'lent men have met,
That for my soul have sought; and thee
  before them have not set.

15 But thou art full of pity, Lord,
  a God most gracious,
Long-suffering, and in thy truth
  and mercy plenteous.
16 O turn to me thy countenance,
  and mercy on me have;
Thy servant strengthen, and the son
  of thine own handmaid save.

17 Shew me a sign for good, that they
  which do me hate may see,
And be asham'd; because thou, Lord,
  didst help and comfort me.

Psalm 87

A Psalm or Song for the sons of Korah.

1 U PON the hills of holiness
    he his foundation sets.

2   God, more than Jacob's dwellings all,
     delights in Sion's gates.
3   Things glorious are said of thee,
     thou city of the Lord.
4   Rahab and Babel I, to those
     that know me, will record:

    Behold ev'n Tyrus, and with it
     the land of Palestine,
    And likewise Ethiopia;
     this man was born therein.
5   And it of Sion shall be said,
     This man and that man there
    Was born; and he that is most High
     himself shall stablish her.

6   When God the people writes, he'll count
     that this man born was there.
7   There be that sing and play; and all
     my well-springs in thee are.

Psalm 88

*A Song or Psalm for the sons of Korah, to the chief Musician
upon Mahalath Leannoth, Maschil of Heman the Ezrahite.*

1   L ORD God, my Saviour, day and night
     before thee cry'd have I.
2   Before thee let my prayer come;
     give ear unto my cry.
3   For troubles great do fill my soul;
     my life draws nigh the grave.
4   I'm counted with those that go down
     to pit, and no strength have.

5   Ev'n free among the dead, like them
     that slain in grave do lie;

Cut off from thy hand, whom no more
    thou hast in memory.
6 Thou hast me laid in lowest pit,
    in deeps and darksome caves.
7 Thy wrath lies hard on me, thou hast
    me press'd with all thy waves.

8 Thou hast put far from me my friends,
    thou mad'st them to abhor me;
And I am so shut up, that I
    find no evasion for me.
9 By reason of affliction
    mine eye mourns dolefully:
To thee, Lord, do I call, and stretch
    my hands continually.

10 Wilt thou shew wonders to the dead?
    shall they rise, and thee bless?
11 Shall in the grave thy love be told?
    in death thy faithfulness?
12 Shall thy great wonders in the dark,
    or shall thy righteousness
Be known to any in the land
    of deep forgetfulness?

13 But, Lord, to thee I cry'd; my pray'r
    at morn prevent shall thee.
14 Why, Lord, dost thou cast off my soul,
    and hid'st thy face from me?
15 Distress'd am I, and from my youth
    I ready am to die;
Thy terrors I have borne, and am
    distracted fearfully.

16 The dreadful fierceness of thy wrath
    quite over me doth go:
Thy terrors great have cut me off,
    they did pursue me so.
17 For round about me ev'ry day,
    like water, they did roll;
And, gathering together, they
    have compassed my soul.

18 My friends thou hast put far from me,
    and him that did me love;
And those that mine acquaintance were
    to darkness didst remove.

Psalm 89

Maschil of Ethan the Ezrahite.

1 GOD'S mercies I will ever sing;
    and with my mouth I shall
Thy faithfulness make to be known
    to generations all.
2 For mercy shall be built, said I,
    for ever to endure;
Thy faithfulness, ev'n in the heav'ns,
    thou wilt establish sure.

3 I with my chosen One have made
    a cov'nant graciously;
And to my servant, whom I lov'd,
    to David sworn have I;
4 That I thy seed establish shall
    for ever to remain,
And will to generations all
    thy throne build and maintain.

5 The praises of thy wonders, Lord,
    the heavens shall express;
And in the congregation
    of saints thy faithfulness.
6 For who in heaven with the Lord
    may once himself compare?
Who is like God among the sons
    of those that mighty are?

7 Great fear in meeting of the saints
    is due unto the Lord;
And he of all about him should
    with rev'rence be ador'd.
8 O thou that art the Lord of hosts,
    what Lord in mightiness
Is like to thee? who compass'd round
    art with thy faithfulness.

9 Ev'n in the raging of the sea
    thou over it dost reign;
And when the waves thereof do swell,
    thou stillest them again.
10 Rahab in pieces thou didst break,
    like one that slaughter'd is;
And with thy mighty arm thou hast
    dispers'd thine enemies.

11 The heav'ns are thine, thou for thine own
    the earth dost also take;
The world, and fulness of the same,
    thy pow'r did found and make.
12 The north and south from thee alone
    their first beginning had;

Both Tabor mount and Hermon hill
    shall in thy name be glad.

13 Thou hast an arm that's full of pow'r,
    thy hand is great in might;
  And thy right hand exceedingly
    exalted is in height.
14 Justice and judgment of thy throne
    are made the dwelling-place;
  Mercy, accompany'd with truth,
    shall go before thy face.

15 O greatly bless'd the people are
    the joyful sound that know;
  In brightness of thy face, O Lord,
    they ever on shall go.
16 They in thy name shall all the day
    rejoice exceedingly;
  And in thy righteousness shall they
    exalted be on high.

17 Because the glory of their strength
    doth only stand in thee;
  And in thy favour shall our horn
    and pow'r exalted be.
18 For God is our defence; and he
    to us doth safety bring:
  The Holy One of Israel
    is our almighty King.

19 In vision to thy Holy One
    thou saidst, I help upon
  A strong one laid; out of the folk
    I rais'd a chosen one;

20 Ev'n David, I have found him out
    a servant unto me;
And with my holy oil my King
    anointed him to be.

21 With whom my hand shall stablish'd be;
    mine arm shall make him strong.
22 On him the foe shall not exact,
    nor son of mischief wrong.
23 I will beat down before his face
    all his malicious foes;
I will them greatly plague who do
    with hatred him oppose.

24 My mercy and my faithfulness
    with him yet still shall be;
And in my name his horn and pow'r
    men shall exalted see.
25 His hand and pow'r shall reach afar,
    I'll set it in the sea;
And his right hand established
    shall in the rivers be.

26 Thou art my Father, he shall cry,
    thou art my God alone;
And he shall say, Thou art the Rock
    of my salvation.
27 I'll make him my first-born, more high
    than kings of any land.
28 My love I'll ever keep for him,
    my cov'nant fast shall stand.

29 His seed I by my pow'r will make
    for ever to endure;

And, as the days of heav'n, his throne
  shall stable be, and sure.
30 But if his children shall forsake
  my laws, and go astray,
And in my judgments shall not walk,
  but wander from my way:

31 If they my laws break, and do not
  keep my commandements;
32 I'll visit then their faults with rods,
  their sins with chastisements.
33 Yet I'll not take my love from him,
  nor false my promise make.
34 My cov'nant I'll not break, nor change
  what with my mouth I spake.

35 Once by my holiness I sware,
  to David I'll not lie;
36 His seed and throne shall, as the sun,
  before me last for aye.
37 It, like the moon, shall ever be
  establish'd stedfastly;
And like to that which in the heav'n
  doth witness faithfully.

38 But thou, displeased, hast cast off,
  thou didst abhor and loathe;
With him that thine anointed is
  thou hast been very wroth.
39 Thou hast thy servant's covenant
  made void, and quite cast by;
Thou hast profan'd his crown, while it
  cast on the ground doth lie.

40 Thou all his hedges hast broke down,
    his strong holds down hast torn.
41 He to all passers-by a spoil,
    to neighbours is a scorn.
42 Thou hast set up his foes' right hand;
    mad'st all his en'mies glad:
43 Turn'd his sword's edge, and him to stand
    in battle hast not made.

44 His glory thou hast made to cease,
    his throne to ground down cast;
45 Shorten'd his days of youth, and him
    with shame thou cover'd hast.
46 How long, Lord, wilt thou hide thyself?
    for ever, in thine ire?
    And shall thine indignation
    burn like unto a fire?

47 Remember, Lord, how short a time
    I shall on earth remain:
    O wherefore is it so that thou
    has made all men in vain?
48 What man is he that liveth here,
    and death shall never see?
    Or from the power of the grave
    what man his soul shall free?

49 Thy former loving-kindnesses,
    O Lord, where be they now?
    Those which in truth and faithfulness
    to David sworn hast thou?
50 Mind, Lord, thy servant's sad reproach;
    how I in bosom bear

The scornings of the people all,
 who strong and mighty are.

51 Wherewith thy raging enemies
   reproach'd, O Lord, think on;
   Wherewith they have reproach'd the steps
   of thine anointed one.
52 All blessing to the Lord our God
   let be ascribed then:
   For evermore so let it be.
   Amen, yea, and amen.

Psalm 90

A Prayer of Moses the man of God.

1 L ORD, thou hast been our dwelling-place
   in generations all.
2 Before thou ever hadst brought forth
   the mountains great or small;
   Ere ever thou hadst form'd the earth,
   and all the world abroad;
   Ev'n thou from everlasting art
   to everlasting God.

3 Thou dost unto destruction
   man that is mortal turn;
   And unto them thou say'st, Again,
   ye sons of men, return.
4 Because a thousand years appear
   no more before thy sight
   Than yesterday, when it is past,
   or than a watch by night.

5 As with an overflowing flood
   thou carry'st them away:

They like a sleep are, like the grass
    that grows at morn are they.
6 At morn it flourishes and grows,
    cut down at ev'n doth fade.
7 For by thine anger we're consum'd,
    thy wrath makes us afraid.

8 Our sins thou and iniquities
    dost in thy presence place,
And sett'st our secret faults before
    the brightness of thy face.
9 For in thine anger all our days
    do pass on to an end;
And as a tale that hath been told,
    so we our years do spend.

10 Threescore and ten years do sum up
    our days and years, we see;
Or, if, by reason of more strength,
    in some fourscore they be:
Yet doth the strength of such old men
    but grief and labour prove;
For it is soon cut off, and we
    fly hence, and soon remove.

11 Who knows the power of thy wrath?
    according to thy fear
12 So is thy wrath: Lord, teach thou us
    our end in mind to bear;
And so to count our days, that we
    our hearts may still apply
To learn thy wisdom and thy truth,
    that we may live thereby.

13 Turn yet again to us, O Lord,
    how long thus shall it be?
Let it repent thee now for those
    that servants are to thee.
14 O with thy tender mercies, Lord,
    us early satisfy;
So we rejoice shall all our days,
    and still be glad in thee.

15 According as the days have been,
    wherein we grief have had,
And years wherein we ill have seen,
    so do thou make us glad.
16 O let thy work and pow'r appear
    thy servants' face before;
And shew unto their children dear
    thy glory evermore:

17 And let the beauty of the Lord
    our God be us upon:
Our handy-works establish thou,
    establish them each one.

Psalm 91

1 HE that doth in the secret place
    of the most High reside,
Under the shade of him that is
    th' Almighty shall abide.
2 I of the Lord my God will say,
    He is my refuge still,
He is my fortress, and my God,
    and in him trust I will.

3 Assuredly he shall thee save,
  and give deliverance
From subtile fowler's snare, and from
  the noisome pestilence.
4 His feathers shall thee hide; thy trust
  under his wings shall be:
His faithfulness shall be a shield
  and buckler unto thee.

5 Thou shalt not need to be afraid
  for terrors of the night;
Nor for the arrow that doth fly
  by day, while it is light;
6 Nor for the pestilence, that walks
  in darkness secretly;
Nor for destruction, that doth waste
  at noon-day openly.

7 A thousand at thy side shall fall,
  on thy right hand shall lie
Ten thousand dead; yet unto thee
  it shall not once come nigh.
8 Only thou with thine eyes shalt look,
  and a beholder be;
And thou therein the just reward
  of wicked men shalt see.

9 Because the Lord, who constantly
  my refuge is alone,
Ev'n the most High, is made by thee
  thy habitation;
10 No plague shall near thy dwelling come;
  no ill shall thee befall:

11 For thee to keep in all thy ways
   his angels charge he shall.

12 They in their hands shall bear thee up,
   still waiting thee upon;
   Lest thou at any time should'st dash
   thy foot against a stone.

13 Upon the adder thou shalt tread,
   and on the lion strong;
   Thy feet on dragons trample shall,
   and on the lions young.

14 Because on me he set his love,
   I'll save and set him free;
   Because my great name he hath known,
   I will him set on high.

15 He'll call on me, I'll answer him;
   I will be with him still
   In trouble, to deliver him,
   and honour him I will.

16 With length of days unto his mind
   I will him satisfy;
   I also my salvation
   will cause his eyes to see.

Psalm 92

A Psalm or Song for the sabbath day.

1 TO render thanks unto the Lord
   it is a comely thing,
   And to thy name, O thou most High,
   due praise aloud to sing.

2 Thy loving-kindness to shew forth
   when shines the morning light;

And to declare thy faithfulness
  with pleasure ev'ry night.

3 On a ten-stringed instrument,
     upon the psaltery,
   And on the harp with solemn sound,
     and grave sweet melody.
4 For thou, Lord, by thy mighty works
     hast made my heart right glad;
   And I will triumph in the works
     which by thine hands were made.

5 How great, Lord, are thy works! each
               thought
     of thine a deep it is:
6 A brutish man it knoweth not;
     fools understand not this.
7 When those that lewd and wicked are
     spring quickly up like grass,
   And workers of iniquity
     do flourish all apace;

   It is that they for ever may
     destroyed be and slain;
8 But thou, O Lord, art the most High,
     for ever to remain.
9 For, lo, thine enemies, O Lord,
     thine en'mies perish shall;
   The workers of iniquity
     shall be dispersed all.

10 But thou shalt, like unto the horn
     of th' unicorn, exalt

My horn on high: thou with fresh oil
    anoint me also shalt.
11 Mine eyes shall also my desire
    see on mine enemies;
Mine ears shall of the wicked hear
    that do against me rise.

12 But like the palm-tree flourishing
    shall be the righteous one;
He shall like to the cedar grow
    that is in Lebanon.
13 Those that within the house of God
    are planted by his grace,
They shall grow up, and flourish all
    in our God's holy place.

14 And in old age, when others fade,
    they fruit still forth shall bring;
They shall be fat, and full of sap,
    and aye be flourishing;
15 To shew that upright is the Lord:
    he is a rock to me;
And he from all unrighteousness
    is altogether free.

Psalm 93

1 THE Lord doth reign, and cloth'd is he
    with majesty most bright;
His works do shew him cloth'd to be,
    and girt about with might.
The world is also stablished,
    that it cannot depart.
2 Thy throne is fix'd of old, and thou
    from everlasting art.

3 The floods, O Lord, have lifted up,
    they lifted up their voice;
The floods have lifted up their waves,
    and made a mighty noise.
4 But yet the Lord, that is on high,
    is more of might by far
Than noise of many waters is,
    or great sea-billows are.

5 Thy testimonies ev'ry one
    in faithfulness excel;
And holiness for ever, Lord,
    thine house becometh well.

Psalm 94

1 O LORD God, unto whom alone
    all vengeance doth belong;
O mighty God, who vengeance own'st,
    shine forth, avenging wrong.
2 Lift up thyself, thou of the earth
    the sov'reign Judge that art;
And unto those that are so proud
    a due reward impart.

3 How long, O mighty God, shall they
    who lewd and wicked be,
How long shall they who wicked are
    thus triumph haughtily?
4 How long shall things most hard by them
    be uttered and told?
And all that work iniquity
    to boast themselves be bold?

5 Thy folk they break in pieces, Lord,
    thine heritage oppress:

6 The widow they and stranger slay,
  and kill the fatherless.
7 Yet say they, God it shall not see,
  nor God of Jacob know.
8 Ye brutish people! understand;
  fools! when wise will ye grow?

9 The Lord did plant the ear of man,
  and hear then shall not he?
  He only form'd the eye, and then
  shall he not clearly see?
10 He that the nations doth correct,
  shall he not chastise you?
  He knowledge unto man doth teach,
  and shall himself not know?

11 Man's thoughts to be but vanity
  the Lord doth well discern.
12 Bless'd is the man thou chast'nest, Lord,
  and mak'st thy law to learn:
13 That thou may'st give him rest from days
  of sad adversity,
  Until the pit be digg'd for those
  that work iniquity.

14 For sure the Lord will not cast off
  those that his people be,
  Neither his own inheritance
  quit and forsake will he:
15 But judgment unto righteousness
  shall yet return again;
  And all shall follow after it
  that are right-hearted men.

16 Who will rise up for me against
    those that do wickedly?
Who will stand up for me 'gainst those
    that work iniquity?
17 Unless the Lord had been my help
    when I was sore opprest,
Almost my soul had in the house
    of silence been at rest.

18 When I had uttered this word,
    my foot doth slip away,
Thy mercy held me up, O Lord,
    thy goodness did me stay.
19 Amidst the multitude of thoughts
    which in my heart do fight,
My soul, lest it be overcharg'd,
    thy comforts do delight.

20 Shall of iniquity the throne
    have fellowship with thee,
Which mischief, cunningly contriv'd,
    doth by a law decree?
21 Against the righteous souls they join,
    they guiltless blood condemn.
22 But of my refuge God's the rock,
    and my defence from them.

23 On them their own iniquity
    the Lord shall bring and lay,
And cut them off in their own sin;
    our Lord God shall them slay.

Psalm 95

1 O COME, let us sing to the Lord:
   come, let us ev'ry one
   A joyful noise make to the Rock
   of our salvation.

2 Let us before his presence come
   with praise and thankful voice;
   Let us sing psalms to him with grace,
   and make a joyful noise.

3 For God, a great God, and great King,
   above all gods he is.

4 Depths of the earth are in his hand,
   the strength of hills is his.

5 To him the spacious sea belongs,
   for he the same did make;
   The dry land also from his hands
   its form at first did take.

6 O come, and let us worship him,
   let us bow down withal,
   And on our knees before the Lord
   our Maker let us fall.

7 For he's our God, the people we
   of his own pasture are,
   And of his hand the sheep; to-day,
   if ye his voice will hear,

8 Then harden not your hearts, as in
   the provocation,
   As in the desert, on the day
   of the tentation:

9 When me your fathers tempt'd and prov'd,
   and did my working see;

10 Ev'n for the space of forty years
   this race hath grieved me.

I said, This people errs in heart,
   my ways they do not know:
11 To whom I sware in wrath, that to
   my rest they should not go.

Psalm 96

1 O SING a new song to the Lord:
   sing all the earth to God.
2 To God sing, bless his name, shew still
   his saving health abroad.
3 Among the heathen nations
   his glory do declare;
   And unto all the people shew
   his works that wondrous are.

4 For great's the Lord, and greatly he
   is to be magnify'd;
   Yea, worthy to be fear'd is he
   above all gods beside.
5 For all the gods are idols dumb,
   which blinded nations fear;
   But our God is the Lord, by whom
   the heav'ns created were.

6 Great honour is before his face,
   and majesty divine;
   Strength is within his holy place,
   and there doth beauty shine.
7 Do ye ascribe unto the Lord,
   of people ev'ry tribe,

Glory do ye unto the Lord,
 and mighty pow'r ascribe.

8 Give ye the glory to the Lord
 that to his name is due;
Come ye into his courts, and bring
 an offering with you.
9 In beauty of his holiness,
 O do the Lord adore;
Likewise let all the earth throughout
 tremble his face before.

10 Among the heathen say, God reigns;
 the world shall stedfastly
Be fix'd from moving; he shall judge
 the people righteously.
11 Let heav'ns be glad before the Lord,
 and let the earth rejoice;
Let seas, and all that is therein,
 cry out, and make a noise.

12 Let fields rejoice, and ev'ry thing
 that springeth of the earth:
Then woods and ev'ry tree shall sing
 with gladness and with mirth
13 Before the Lord; because he comes,
 to judge the earth comes he:
He'll judge the world with righteousness,
 the people faithfully.

Psalm 97

1 GOD reigneth, let the earth be glad,
 and isles rejoice each one.

2 Dark clouds him compass; and in right
    with judgment dwells his throne.
3 Fire goes before him, and his foes
    it burns up round about:
4 His lightnings lighten did the world;
    earth saw, and shook throughout.

5 Hills at the presence of the Lord,
    like wax, did melt away;
    Ev'n at the presence of the Lord
    of all the earth, I say.
6 The heav'ns declare his righteousness,
    all men his glory see.
7 All who serve graven images,
    confounded let them be.

Who do of idols boast themselves,
    let shame upon them fall:
Ye that are called gods, see that
    ye do him worship all.
8 Sion did hear, and joyful was,
    glad Judah's daughters were;
They much rejoic'd, O Lord, because
    thy judgments did appear.

9 For thou, O Lord, art high above
    all things on earth that are;
    Above all other gods thou art
    exalted very far.
10 Hate ill, all ye that love the Lord:
    his saints' souls keepeth he;
    And from the hands of wicked men
    he sets them safe and free.

11 For all those that be righteous
    sown is a joyful light,
And gladness sown is for all those
    that are in heart upright.
12 Ye righteous, in the Lord rejoice;
    express your thankfulness,
When ye into your memory
    do call his holiness.

Psalm 98

A Psalm.

1 O SING a new song to the Lord,
    for wonders he hath done:
His right hand and his holy arm
    him victory hath won.
2 The Lord God his salvation
    hath caused to be known;
His justice in the heathen's sight
    he openly hath shown.

3 He mindful of his grace and truth
    to Isr'el's house hath been;
And the salvation of our God
    all ends of th' earth have seen.
4 Let all the earth unto the Lord
    send forth a joyful noise;
Lift up your voice aloud to him,
    sing praises, and rejoice.

5 With harp, with harp, and voice of psalms,
    unto JEHOVAH sing:
6 With trumpets, cornets, gladly sound
    before the Lord the King.

7 Let seas and all their fulness roar;
    the world, and dwellers there;
8 Let floods clap hands, and let the hills
    together joy declare

9 Before the Lord; because he comes,
    to judge the earth comes he:
He'll judge the world with righteousness,
    his folk with equity.

Psalm 99

1 TH' eternal Lord doth reign as king,
    let all the people quake;
He sits between the cherubims,
    let th' earth be mov'd and shake.
2 The Lord in Sion great and high
    above all people is;
3 Thy great and dreadful name (for it
    is holy) let them bless.

4 The king's strength also judgment loves;
    thou settlest equity:
Just judgment thou dost execute
    in Jacob righteously.
5 The Lord our God exalt on high,
    and rev'rently do ye
Before his footstool worship him:
    the Holy One is he.

6 Moses and Aaron 'mong his priests,
    Samuel, with them that call
Upon his name: these call'd on God,
    and he them answer'd all.

7   Within the pillar of the cloud
      he unto them did speak:
   The testimonies he them taught,
      and laws, they did not break.

8   Thou answer'dst them, O Lord our God;
      thou wast a God that gave
   Pardon to them, though on their deeds
      thou wouldest vengeance have.
9   Do ye exalt the Lord our God,
      and at his holy hill
   Do ye him worship: for the Lord
      our God is holy still.

Psalm 100

A Psalm of praise.

1   ALL people that on earth do dwell,
      Sing to the Lord with cheerful voice.
2   Him serve with mirth, his praise forth tell,
      Come ye before him and rejoice.
3   Know that the Lord is God indeed;
      Without our aid he did us make:
   We are his flock, he doth us feed,
      And for his sheep he doth us take.

4   O enter then his gates with praise,
      Approach with joy his courts unto:
   Praise, laud, and bless his name always,
      For it is seemly so to do.
5   For why? the Lord our God is good,
      His mercy is for ever sure;
   His truth at all times firmly stood,
      And shall from age to age endure.

Another of the same

1 O ALL ye lands, unto the Lord
  make ye a joyful noise.
2 Serve God with gladness, him before
  come with a singing voice.
3 Know ye the Lord that he is God;
  not we, but he us made:
  We are his people, and the sheep
  within his pasture fed.

4 Enter his gates and courts with praise,
  to thank him go ye thither:
  To him express your thankfulness,
  and bless his name together.
5 Because the Lord our God is good,
  his mercy faileth never;
  And to all generations
  his truth endureth ever.

Psalm 101

A Psalm of David.

1 I MERCY will and judgment sing,
  Lord, I will sing to thee.
2 With wisdom in a perfect way
  shall my behaviour be.
  O when, in kindness unto me,
  wilt thou be pleas'd to come?
  I with a perfect heart will walk
  within my house at home.

3 I will endure no wicked thing
  before mine eyes to be:

I hate their work that turn aside,
    it shall not cleave to me.
4 A stubborn and a froward heart
    depart quite from me shall;
A person giv'n to wickedness
    I will not know at all.

5 I'll cut him off that slandereth
    his neighbour privily:
The haughty heart I will not bear,
    nor him that looketh high.
6 Upon the faithful of the land
    mine eyes shall be, that they
May dwell with me: he shall me serve
    that walks in perfect way.

7 Who of deceit a worker is
    in my house shall not dwell;
And in my presence shall he not
    remain that lies doth tell.
8 Yea, all the wicked of the land
    early destroy will I;
All from God's city to cut off
    that work iniquity.

Psalm 102

*A Prayer of the afflicted, when he is overwhelmed,
and poureth out his complaint before the Lord.*

1 O LORD, unto my pray'r give ear,
    my cry let come to thee;
2 And in the day of my distress
    hide not thy face from me.

Give ear to me; what time I call,
    to answer me make haste:
3 For, as an hearth, my bones are burnt,
    my days, like smoke, do waste.

4 My heart within me smitten is,
    and it is withered
Like very grass; so that I do
    forget to eat my bread.
5 By reason of my groaning voice
    my bones cleave to my skin.
6 Like pelican in wilderness
    forsaken I have been:

I like an owl in desert am,
    that nightly there doth moan;
7 I watch, and like a sparrow am
    on the house-top alone.
8 My bitter en'mies all the day
    reproaches cast on me;
And, being mad at me, with rage
    against me sworn they be.

9 For why? I ashes eaten have
    like bread, in sorrows deep;
My drink I also mingled have
    with tears that I did weep.
10 Thy wrath and indignation
    did cause this grief and pain;
For thou hast lift me up on high,
    and cast me down again.

11 My days are like unto a shade,
    which doth declining pass;

And I am dry'd and withered,
  ev'n like unto the grass.
12 But thou, Lord, everlasting art,
  and thy remembrance shall
Continually endure, and be
  to generations all.

13 Thou shalt arise, and mercy have
  upon thy Sion yet;
The time to favour her is come,
  the time that thou hast set.
14 For in her rubbish and her stones
  thy servants pleasure take;
Yea, they the very dust thereof
  do favour for her sake.

15 So shall the heathen people fear
  the Lord's most holy name;
And all the kings on earth shall dread
  thy glory and thy fame.
16 When Sion by the mighty Lord
  built up again shall be,
In glory then and majesty
  to men appear shall he.

17 The prayer of the destitute
  he surely will regard;
Their prayer will he not despise,
  by him it shall be heard.
18 For generations yet to come
  this shall be on record:
So shall the people that shall be
  created praise the Lord.

19 He from his sanctuary's height
    hath downward cast his eye;
And from his glorious throne in heav'n
    the Lord the earth did spy;
20 That of the mournful prisoner
    the groanings he might hear,
To set them free that unto death
    by men appointed are:

21 That they in Sion may declare
    the Lord's most holy name,
And publish in Jerusalem
    the praises of the same;
22 When as the people gather shall
    in troops with one accord,
When kingdoms shall assembled be
    to serve the highest Lord.

23 My wonted strength and force he hath
    abated in the way,
And he my days hath shortened:
24   Thus therefore did I say,
My God, in mid-time of my days
    take thou me not away:
From age to age eternally
    thy years endure and stay.

25 The firm foundation of the earth
    of old time thou hast laid;
The heavens also are the work
    which thine own hands have made.
26 Thou shalt for evermore endure,
    but they shall perish all;

Yea, ev'ry one of them wax old,
   like to a garment, shall:

Thou, as a vesture, shalt them change,
   and they shall changed be:
27 But thou the same art, and thy years
   are to eternity.
28 The children of thy servants shall
   continually endure;
And in thy sight, O Lord, their seed
   shall be establish'd sure.

Another of the same

1 LORD, hear my pray'r, and let my cry
   Have speedy access unto thee;
2 In day of my calamity
   O hide not thou thy face from me.
Hear when I call to thee; that day
   An answer speedily return:
3 My days, like smoke, consume away,
   And, as an hearth, my bones do burn.

4 My heart is wounded very sore,
   And withered, like grass doth fade:
I am forgetful grown therefore
   To take and eat my daily bread.
5 By reason of my smart within,
   And voice of my most grievous groans,
My flesh consumed is, my skin,
   All parch'd, doth cleave unto my bones.

6 The pelican of wilderness,
   The owl in desert, I do match;
7 And, sparrow-like, companionless,
   Upon the house's top, I watch.

8   I all day long am made a scorn,
     Reproach'd by my malicious foes:
    The madmen are against me sworn,
     The men against me that arose.

9   For I have ashes eaten up,
     To me as if they had been bread;
    And with my drink I in my cup
     Of bitter tears a mixture made.

10 Because thy wrath was not appeas'd,
     And dreadful indignation:
    Therefore it was that thou me rais'd,
     And thou again didst cast me down.

11 My days are like a shade alway,
     Which doth declining swiftly pass;
    And I am withered away,
     Much like unto the fading grass.

12 But thou, O Lord, shalt still endure,
     From change and all mutation free,
    And to all generations sure
     Shall thy remembrance ever be.

13 Thou shalt arise, and mercy yet
     Thou to mount Sion shalt extend:
    Her time for favour which was set,
     Behold, is now come to an end.

14 Thy saints take pleasure in her stones,
     Her very dust to them is dear.

15 All heathen lands and kingly thrones
     On earth thy glorious name shall fear.

16 God in his glory shall appear,
     When Sion he builds and repairs.

17 He shall regard and lend his ear
 Unto the needy's humble pray'rs:
 Th' afflicted's pray'r he will not scorn.
18 All times this shall be on record:
 And generations yet unborn
 Shall praise and magnify the Lord.

19 He from his holy place look'd down,
 The earth he view'd from heav'n on high,
20 To hear the pris'ner's mourning groan,
 And free them that are doom'd to die;
21 That Sion, and Jerus'lem too,
 His name and praise may well record,
22 When people and the kingdoms do
 Assemble all to praise the Lord.

23 My strength he weaken'd in the way,
 My days of life he shortened.
24 My God, O take me not away
 In mid-time of my days, I said:
 Thy years throughout all ages last.
25 Of old thou hast established
 The earth's foundation firm and fast:
 Thy mighty hands the heav'ns have made.

26 They perish shall, as garments do,
 But thou shalt evermore endure;
 As vestures, thou shalt change them so;
 And they shall all be changed sure:
27 But from all changes thou art free;
 Thy endless years do last for aye.
28 Thy servants, and their seed who be,
 Establish'd shall before thee stay.

Psalm 103

A Psalm of David.

1 O THOU my soul, bless God the Lord;
    and all that in me is
  Be stirred up his holy name
    to magnify and bless.
2 Bless, O my soul, the Lord thy God,
    and not forgetful be
  Of all his gracious benefits
    he hath bestow'd on thee.

3 All thine iniquities who doth
    most graciously forgive:
  Who thy diseases all and pains
    doth heal, and thee relieve.
4 Who doth redeem thy life, that thou
    to death may'st not go down;
  Who thee with loving-kindness doth
    and tender mercies crown:

5 Who with abundance of good things
    doth satisfy thy mouth;
  So that, ev'n as the eagle's age,
    renewed is thy youth.
6 God righteous judgment executes
    for all oppressed ones.
7 His ways to Moses, he his acts
    made known to Isr'el's sons.

8 The Lord our God is merciful,
    and he is gracious,
  Long-suffering, and slow to wrath,
    in mercy plenteous.

9 He will not chide continually,
    nor keep his anger still.
10 With us he dealt not as we sinn'd,
    nor did requite our ill.

11 For as the heaven in its height
    the earth surmounteth far:
  So great to those that do him fear
    his tender mercies are:
12 As far as east is distant from
    the west, so far hath he
  From us removed, in his love,
    all our iniquity.

13 Such pity as a father hath
    unto his children dear;
  Like pity shews the Lord to such
    as worship him in fear.
14 For he remembers we are dust,
    and he our frame well knows.
15 Frail man, his days are like the grass,
    as flow'r in field he grows:

16 For over it the wind doth pass,
    and it away is gone;
  And of the place where once it was
    it shall no more be known.
17 But unto them that do him fear
    God's mercy never ends;
  And to their children's children still
    his righteousness extends:

18 To such as keep his covenant,
    and mindful are alway

Of his most just commandements,
    that they may them obey.
19 The Lord prepared hath his throne
    in heavens firm to stand;
  And ev'ry thing that being hath
    his kingdom doth command.

20 O ye his angels, that excel
    in strength, bless ye the Lord;
  Ye who obey what he commands,
    and hearken to his word.
21 O bless and magnify the Lord,
    ye glorious hosts of his;
  Ye ministers, that do fulfil
    whate'er his pleasure is.

22 O bless the Lord, all ye his works,
    wherewith the world is stor'd
  In his dominions ev'ry where.
    My soul, bless thou the Lord.

Psalm 104

1 BLESS God, my soul. O Lord my God,
    thou art exceeding great;
  With honour and with majesty
    thou clothed art in state.
2 With light, as with a robe, thyself
    thou coverest about;
  And, like unto a curtain, thou
    the heavens stretchest out.

3 Who of his chambers doth the beams
    within the waters lay;

Who doth the clouds his chariot make,
   on wings of wind make way.
4 Who flaming fire his ministers,
   his angels sp'rits, doth make:
5 Who earth's foundations did lay,
   that it should never shake.

6 Thou didst it cover with the deep,
   as with a garment spread:
The waters stood above the hills,
   when thou the word but said.
7 But at the voice of thy rebuke
   they fled, and would not stay;
They at thy thunder's dreadful voice
   did haste them fast away.

8 They by the mountains do ascend,
   and by the valley-ground
Descend, unto that very place
   which thou for them didst found.
9 Thou hast a bound unto them set,
   that they may not pass over,
That they do not return again
   the face of earth to cover.

10 He to the valleys sends the springs,
   which run among the hills:
11 They to all beasts of field give drink,
   wild asses drink their fills.
12 By them the fowls of heav'n shall have
   their habitation,
Which do among the branches sing
   with delectation.

13 He from his chambers watereth
 the hills, when they are dry'd:
With fruit and increase of thy works
 the earth is satisfy'd.
14 For cattle he makes grass to grow,
 he makes the herb to spring
For th' use of man, that food to him
 he from the earth may bring;

15 And wine, that to the heart of man
 doth cheerfulness impart,
Oil that his face makes shine, and bread
 that strengtheneth his heart.
16 The trees of God are full of sap;
 the cedars that do stand
In Lebanon, which planted were
 by his almighty hand.

17 Birds of the air upon their boughs
 do chuse their nests to make;
As for the stork, the fir-tree she
 doth for her dwelling take.
18 The lofty mountains for wild goats
 a place of refuge be;
The conies also to the rocks
 do for their safety flee.

19 He sets the moon in heav'n, thereby
 the seasons to discern:
From him the sun his certain time
 of going down doth learn.
20 Thou darkness mak'st, 'tis night, then beasts
 of forests creep abroad.
21 The lions young roar for their prey,
 and seek their meat from God.

22 The sun doth rise, and home they flock,
    down in their dens they lie.
23 Man goes to work, his labour he
    doth to the ev'ning ply.
24 How manifold, Lord, are thy works!
    in wisdom wonderful
Thou ev'ry one of them hast made;
    earth's of thy riches full:

25 So is this great and spacious sea,
    wherein things creeping are,
Which number'd cannot be; and beasts
    both great and small are there.
26 There ships go; there thou mak'st to play
    that leviathan great.
27 These all wait on thee, that thou may'st
    in due time give them meat.

28 That which thou givest unto them
    they gather for their food;
Thine hand thou open'st lib'rally,
    they filled are with good.
29 Thou hid'st thy face; they troubled are,
    their breath thou tak'st away;
Then do they die, and to their dust
    return again do they.

30 Thy quick'ning spirit thou send'st forth,
    then they created be;
And then the earth's decayed face
    renewed is by thee.
31 The glory of the mighty Lord
    continue shall for ever:

The Lord JEHOVAH shall rejoice
  in all his works together.

32 Earth, as affrighted, trembleth all,
    if he on it but look;
  And if the mountains he but touch,
    they presently do smoke.
33 I will sing to the Lord most high,
    so long as I shall live;
  And while I being have I shall
    to my God praises give.

34 Of him my meditation shall
    sweet thoughts to me afford;
  And as for me, I will rejoice
    in God, my only Lord.
35 From earth let sinners be consum'd,
    let ill men no more be.
  O thou my soul, bless thou the Lord.
    Praise to the Lord give ye.

Psalm 105

1 GIVE thanks to God, call on his name;
  to men his deeds make known.
2 Sing ye to him, sing psalms; proclaim
  his wondrous works each one.
3 See that ye in his holy name
    to glory do accord;
  And let the heart of ev'ry one
    rejoice that seeks the Lord.

4 The Lord Almighty, and his strength,
  with stedfast hearts seek ye:

His blessed and his gracious face
  seek ye continually.
5 Think on the works that he hath done,
  which admiration breed;
His wonders, and the judgments all
  which from his mouth proceed;

6 O ye that are of Abr'ham's race,
  his servant well approv'n;
And ye that Jacob's children are,
  whom he chose for his own.
7 Because he, and he only, is
  the mighty Lord our God;
And his most righteous judgments are
  in all the earth abroad.

8 His cov'nant he remember'd hath,
  that it may ever stand:
To thousand generations
  the word he did command.
9 Which covenant he firmly made
  with faithful Abraham,
And unto Isaac, by his oath,
  he did renew the same:

10 And unto Jacob, for a law,
  he made it firm and sure,
A covenant to Israel,
  which ever should endure.
11 He said, I'll give Canaan's land
  for heritage to you;
12 While they were strangers there, and few,
  in number very few:

13 While yet they went from land to land
    without a sure abode;
And while through sundry kingdoms they
    did wander far abroad;
14 Yet, notwithstanding, suffer'd he
    no man to do them wrong;
Yea, for their sakes, he did reprove
    kings, who were great and strong.

15 Thus did he say, Touch ye not those
    that mine anointed be,
Nor do the prophets any harm
    that do pertain to me.
16 He call'd for famine on the land,
    he brake the staff of bread:
17 But yet he sent a man before,
    by whom they should be fed;

Ev'n Joseph, whom unnat'rally
    sell for a slave did they;
18 Whose feet with fetters they did hurt,
    and he in irons lay;
19 Until the time that his word came
    to give him liberty;
The word and purpose of the Lord
    did him in prison try.

20 Then sent the king, and did command
    that he enlarg'd should be:
He that the people's ruler was
    did send to set him free.
21 A lord to rule his family
    he rais'd him, as most fit;

To him of all that he possess'd
he did the charge commit:

22 That he might at his pleasure bind
the princes of the land;
And he might teach his senators
wisdom to understand.
23 The people then of Israel
down into Egypt came;
And Jacob also sojourned
within the land of Ham.

24 And he did greatly by his pow'r
increase his people there;
And stronger than their enemies
they by his blessing were.
25 Their heart he turned to envy
his folk maliciously,
With those that his own servants were
to deal in subtilty.

26 His servant Moses he did send,
Aaron his chosen one.
27 By these his signs and wonders great
in Ham's land were made known.
28 Darkness he sent, and made it dark;
his word they did obey.
29 He turn'd their waters into blood,
and he their fish did slay.

30 The land in plenty brought forth frogs
in chambers of their kings.
31 His word all sorts of flies and lice
in all their borders brings.

32 He hail for rain, and flaming fire
    into their land he sent:
33 And he their vines and fig-trees smote;
    trees of their coasts he rent.

34 He spake, and caterpillars came,
    locusts did much abound;
35 Which in their land all herbs consum'd,
    and all fruits of their ground.
36 He smote all first-born in their land,
    chief of their strength each one.
37 With gold and silver brought them forth,
    weak in their tribes were none.

38 Egypt was glad when forth they went,
    their fear on them did light.
39 He spread a cloud for covering,
    and fire to shine by night.
40 They ask'd, and he brought quails: with bread
    of heav'n he filled them.
41 He open'd rocks, floods gush'd, and ran
    in deserts like a stream.

42 For on his holy promise he,
    and servant Abr'ham, thought.
43 With joy his people, his elect
    with gladness, forth he brought.
44 And unto them the pleasant lands
    he of the heathen gave;
    That of the people's labour they
    inheritance might have.

45 That they his statutes might observe
    according to his word;

And that they might his laws obey.
Give praise unto the Lord.

Psalm 106

1   GIVE praise and thanks unto the Lord,
    for bountiful is he;
His tender mercy doth endure
    unto eternity.

2   God's mighty works who can express?
    or shew forth all his praise?

3   Blessed are they that judgment keep,
    and justly do always.

4   Remember me, Lord, with that love
    which thou to thine dost bear;
With thy salvation, O my God,
    to visit me draw near:

5   That I thy chosen's good may see,
    and in their joy rejoice;
And may with thine inheritance
    triumph with cheerful voice.

6   We with our fathers sinned have,
    and of iniquity
Too long we have the workers been;
    we have done wickedly.

7   The wonders great, which thou, O Lord,
    didst work in Egypt land,
Our fathers, though they saw, yet them
    they did not understand:

And they thy mercies' multitude
    kept not in memory;

But at the sea, ev'n the Red sea,
  provok'd him grievously.
8 Nevertheless he saved them,
  ev'n for his own name's sake;
That so he might to be well known
  his mighty power make.

9 When he the Red sea did rebuke,
  then dried up it was:
Through depths, as through the wilderness,
  he safely made them pass.
10 From hands of those that hated them
  he did his people save;
And from the en'my's cruel hand
  to them redemption gave.

11 The waters overwhelm'd their foes;
  not one was left alive.
12 Then they believ'd his word, and praise
  to him in songs did give.
13 But soon did they his mighty works
  forget unthankfully,
And on his counsel and his will
  did not wait patiently;

14 But much did lust in wilderness,
  and God in desert tempt.
15 He gave them what they sought, but to
  their soul he leanness sent.
16 And against Moses in the camp
  their envy did appear;
At Aaron they, the saint of God,
  envious also were.

17 Therefore the earth did open wide,
    and Dathan did devour,
And all Abiram's company
    did cover in that hour.
18 Likewise among their company
    a fire was kindled then;
And so the hot consuming flame
    burnt up these wicked men.

19 Upon the hill of Horeb they
    an idol-calf did frame,
A molten image they did make,
    and worshipped the same.
20 And thus their glory, and their God,
    most vainly changed they
Into the likeness of an ox
    that eateth grass or hay.

21 They did forget the mighty God,
    that had their saviour been,
By whom such great things brought to pass
    they had in Egypt seen.
22 In Ham's land he did wondrous works,
    things terrible did he,
When he his mighty hand and arm
    stretch'd out at the Red sea.

23 Then said he, He would them destroy,
    had not, his wrath to stay,
His chosen Moses stood in breach,
    that them he should not slay.
24 Yea, they despis'd the pleasant land,
    believed not his word:

25 But in their tents they murmured,
  not heark'ning to the Lord.

26 Therefore in desert them to slay
  he lifted up his hand:
27 'Mong nations to o'erthrow their seed,
  and scatter in each land.
28 They unto Baal-peor did
  themselves associate;
The sacrifices of the dead
  they did profanely eat.

29 Thus, by their lewd inventions,
  they did provoke his ire;
And then upon them suddenly
  the plague brake in as fire.
30 Then Phin'has rose, and justice did,
  and so the plague did cease;
31 That to all ages counted was
  to him for righteousness.

32 And at the waters, where they strove,
  they did him angry make,
In such sort, that it fared ill
  with Moses for their sake:
33 Because they there his spirit meek
  provoked bitterly,
So that he utter'd with his lips
  words unadvisedly.

34 Nor, as the Lord commanded them,
  did they the nations slay:
35 But with the heathen mingled were,
  and learn'd of them their way.

36 And they their idols serv'd, which did
    a snare unto them turn.
37 Their sons and daughters they to dev'ls
    in sacrifice did burn.

38 In their own children's guiltless blood
    their hands they did imbrue,
Whom to Canaan's idols they
    for sacrifices slew:
So was the land defil'd with blood.
39   They stain'd with their own way,
And with their own inventions
    a whoring they did stray.

40 Against his people kindled was
    the wrath of God therefore,
Insomuch that he did his own
    inheritance abhor.
41 He gave them to the heathen's hand;
    their foes did them command.
42 Their en'mies them oppress'd, they were
    made subject to their hand.

43 He many times deliver'd them;
    but with their counsel so
They him provok'd, that for their sin
    they were brought very low.
44 Yet their affliction he beheld,
    when he did hear their cry:
45 And he for them his covenant
    did call to memory;

After his mercies' multitude
46   he did repent: And made

Them to be pitied of all those
    who did them captive lead.
47 O Lord our God, us save, and gather
    the heathen from among,
That we thy holy name may praise
    in a triumphant song.

48 Bless'd be JEHOVAH, Isr'el's God,
    to all eternity:
Let all the people say, Amen.
    Praise to the Lord give ye.

Psalm 107

1   **P**RAISE God, for he is good: for still
    his mercies lasting be.
2 Let God's redeem'd say so, whom he
    from th' en'my's hand did free;
3 And gather'd them out of the lands,
    from north, south, east, and west.
4 They stray'd in desert's pathless way,
    no city found to rest.

5 For thirst and hunger in them faints
6   their soul. When straits them press,
They cry unto the Lord, and he
    them frees from their distress.
7 Them also in a way to walk
    that right is he did guide,
That they might to a city go,
    wherein they might abide.

8 O that men to the Lord would give
    praise for his goodness then,

And for his works of wonder done
    unto the sons of men!
9 For he the soul that longing is
    doth fully satisfy;
With goodness he the hungry soul
    doth fill abundantly.

10 Such as shut up in darkness deep,
    and in death's shade abide,
Whom strongly hath affliction bound,
    and irons fast have ty'd:
11 Because against the words of God
    they wrought rebelliously,
And they the counsel did contemn
    of him that is most High:

12 Their heart he did bring down with grief,
    they fell, no help could have.
13 In trouble then they cry'd to God,
    he them from straits did save.
14 He out of darkness did them bring,
    and from death's shade them take;
These bands, wherewith they had been
        bound,
    asunder quite he brake.

15 O that men to the Lord would give
    praise for his goodness then,
And for his works of wonder done
    unto the sons of men!
16 Because the mighty gates of brass
    in pieces he did tear,
By him in sunder also cut
    the bars of iron were.

17 Fools, for their sin, and their offence,
    do sore affliction bear;
18 All kind of meat their soul abhors;
    they to death's gates draw near.
19 In grief they cry to God; he saves
    them from their miseries.
20 He sends his word, them heals, and them
    from their destructions frees.

21 O that men to the Lord would give
    praise for his goodness then,
And for his works of wonder done
    unto the sons of men!
22 And let them sacrifice to him
    off'rings of thankfulness;
And let them shew abroad his works
    in songs of joyfulness.

23 Who go to sea in ships, and in
    great waters trading be,
24 Within the deep these men God's works
    and his great wonders see.
25 For he commands, and forth in haste
    the stormy tempest flies,
Which makes the sea with rolling waves
    aloft to swell and rise.

26 They mount to heav'n, then to the depths
    they do go down again;
Their soul doth faint and melt away
    with trouble and with pain.
27 They reel and stagger like one drunk,
    at their wit's end they be:

28 Then they to God in trouble cry,
    who them from straits doth free.

29 The storm is chang'd into a calm
    at his command and will;
So that the waves, which rag'd before,
    now quiet are and still.
30 Then are they glad, because at rest
    and quiet now they be:
So to the haven he them brings,
    which they desir'd to see.

31 O that men to the Lord would give
    praise for his goodness then,
And for his works of wonder done
    unto the sons of men!
32 Among the people gathered
    let them exalt his name;
Among assembled elders spread
    his most renowned fame.

33 He to dry land turns water-springs,
    and floods to wilderness;
34 For sins of those that dwell therein,
    fat land to barrenness.
35 The burnt and parched wilderness
    to water-pools he brings;
The ground that was dry'd up before
    he turns to water-springs:

36 And there, for dwelling, he a place
    doth to the hungry give,
That they a city may prepare
    commodiously to live.

37 There sow they fields, and vineyards plant,
    to yield fruits of increase.
38 His blessing makes them multiply,
    lets not their beasts decrease.

39 Again they are diminished,
    and very low brought down,
Through sorrow and affliction,
    and great oppression.
40 He upon princes pours contempt
    and causeth them to stray,
And wander in a wilderness,
    wherein there is no way.

41 Yet setteth he the poor on high
    from all his miseries,
And he, much like unto a flock,
    doth make him families.
42 They that are righteous shall rejoice,
    when they the same shall see;
And, as ashamed, stop her mouth
    shall all iniquity.

43 Whoso is wise, and will these things
    observe, and them record,
Ev'n they shall understand the love
    and kindness of the Lord.

Psalm 108

A Song or Psalm of David.

1 MY heart is fix'd, Lord; I will sing,
    and with my glory praise.
2 Awake up psaltery and harp;
    myself I'll early raise.

3 I'll praise thee 'mong the people, Lord;
 'mong nations sing will I:
4 For above heav'n thy mercy's great,
 thy truth doth reach the sky.

5 Be thou above the heavens, Lord,
 exalted gloriously;
Thy glory all the earth above
 be lifted up on high.
6 That those who thy beloved are
 delivered may be,
O do thou save with thy right hand,
 and answer give to me.

7 God in his holiness hath said,
 Herein I will take pleasure;
Shechem I will divide, and forth
 will Succoth's valley measure.
8 Gilead I claim as mine by right;
 Manasseh mine shall be;
Ephraim is of my head the strength;
 Judah gives laws for me;

9 Moab's my washing-pot; my shoe
 I'll over Edom throw;
Over the land of Palestine
 I will in triumph go.
10 O who is he will bring me to
 the city fortify'd?
O who is he that to the land
 of Edom will me guide?

11 O God, thou who hadst cast us off,
 this thing wilt thou not do?

And wilt not thou, ev'n thou, O God,
    forth with our armies go?
12 Do thou from trouble give us help,
    for helpless is man's aid.
13 Through God we shall do valiantly;
    our foes he shall down tread.

Psalm 109

To the chief Musician, A Psalm of David.

1 O THOU the God of all my praise,
    do thou not hold thy peace;
2 For mouths of wicked men to speak
    against me do not cease:
The mouths of vile deceitful men
    against me open'd be;
And with a false and lying tongue
    they have accused me.

3 They did beset me round about
    with words of hateful spite:
And though to them no cause I gave,
    against me they did fight.
4 They for my love became my foes,
    but I me set to pray.
5 Evil for good, hatred for love,
    to me they did repay.

6 Set thou the wicked over him;
    and upon his right hand
Give thou his greatest enemy,
    ev'n Satan, leave to stand.
7 And when by thee he shall be judg'd,
    let him condemned be;

And let his pray'r be turn'd to sin,
    when he shall call on thee.

8 Few be his days, and in his room
     his charge another take.
9 His children let be fatherless,
     his wife a widow make.
10 His children let be vagabonds,
     and beg continually;
  And from their places desolate
     seek bread for their supply.

11 Let covetous extortioners
     catch all he hath away:
  Of all for which he labour'd hath
     let strangers make a prey.
12 Let there be none to pity him,
     let there be none at all
  That on his children fatherless
     will let his mercy fall.

13 Let his posterity from earth
     cut off for ever be,
  And in the foll'wing age their name
     be blotted out by thee.
14 Let God his father's wickedness
     still to remembrance call;
  And never let his mother's sin
     be blotted out at all.

15 But let them all before the Lord
     appear continually,
  That he may wholly from the earth
     cut off their memory.

16 Because he mercy minded not,
    but persecuted still
The poor and needy, that he might
    the broken-hearted kill.

17 As he in cursing pleasure took,
    so let it to him fall;
As he delighted not to bless,
    so bless him not at all.
18 As cursing he like clothes put on,
    into his bowels so,
Like water, and into his bones,
    like oil, down let it go.

19 Like to the garment let it be
    which doth himself array,
And for a girdle, wherewith he
    is girt about alway.
20 From God let this be their reward
    that en'mies are to me,
And their reward that speak against
    my soul maliciously.

21 But do thou, for thine own name's sake,
    O God the Lord, for me:
Sith good and sweet thy mercy is,
    from trouble set me free.
22 For I am poor and indigent,
    afflicted sore am I,
My heart within me also is
    wounded exceedingly.

23 I pass like a declining shade,
    am like the locust tost:

24 My knees through fasting weaken'd are,
   my flesh hath fatness lost.
25 I also am a vile reproach
   unto them made to be;
   And they that did upon me look
   did shake their heads at me.

26 O do thou help and succour me,
   who art my God and Lord:
   And, for thy tender mercy's sake,
   safety to me afford:
27 That thereby they may know that this
   is thy almighty hand;
   And that thou, Lord, hast done the same,
   they may well understand.

28 Although they curse with spite, yet, Lord,
   bless thou with loving voice:
   Let them asham'd be when they rise;
   thy servant let rejoice.
29 Let thou mine adversaries all
   with shame be clothed over;
   And let their own confusion
   them, as a mantle, cover.

30 But as for me, I with my mouth
   will greatly praise the Lord;
   And I among the multitude
   his praises will record.
31 For he shall stand at his right hand
   who is in poverty,
   To save him from all those that would
   condemn his soul to die.

Psalm 110

A Psalm of David.

1 THE Lord did say unto my Lord,
    Sit thou at my right hand,
Until I make thy foes a stool,
    whereon thy feet may stand.
2 The Lord shall out of Sion send
    the rod of thy great pow'r:
In midst of all thine enemies
    be thou the governor.

3 A willing people in thy day
    of pow'r shall come to thee,
In holy beauties from morn's womb;
    thy youth like dew shall be.
4 The Lord himself hath made an oath,
    and will repent him never,
Of th' order of Melchisedec
    thou art a priest for ever.

5 The glorious and mighty Lord,
    that sits at thy right hand,
Shall, in his day of wrath, strike through
    kings that do him withstand.
6 He shall among the heathen judge,
    he shall with bodies dead
The places fill: o'er many lands
    he wound shall ev'ry head.

7 The brook that runneth in the way
    with drink shall him supply;
And, for this cause, in triumph he
    shall lift his head on high.

Psalm 111

1 PRAISE ye the Lord: with my whole
        heart
  I will God's praise declare,
  Where the assemblies of the just
    and congregations are.
2 The whole works of the Lord our God
    are great above all measure,
  Sought out they are of ev'ry one
    that doth therein take pleasure.

3 His work most honourable is,
    most glorious and pure,
  And his untainted righteousness
    for ever doth endure.
4 His works most wonderful he hath
    made to be thought upon:
  The Lord is gracious, and he is
    full of compassion.

5 He giveth meat unto all those
    that truly do him fear;
  And evermore his covenant
    he in his mind will bear.
6 He did the power of his works
    unto his people show,
  When he the heathen's heritage
    upon them did bestow.

7 His handy-works are truth and right;
    all his commands are sure:
8 And, done in truth and uprightness,
    they evermore endure.

9　He sent redemption to his folk;
　　　his covenant for aye
　　He did command: holy his name
　　　and rev'rend is alway.

10　Wisdom's beginning is God's fear:
　　　good understanding they
　　Have all that his commands fulfill:
　　　his praise endures for aye.

Psalm 112

1　**P**RAISE ye the Lord. The man is bless'd
　　that fears the Lord aright,
　　He who in his commandements
　　　doth greatly take delight.
2　His seed and offspring powerful
　　　shall be the earth upon:
　　Of upright men blessed shall be
　　　the generation.

3　Riches and wealth shall ever be
　　　within his house in store;
　　And his unspotted righteousness
　　　endures for evermore.
4　Unto the upright light doth rise,
　　　though he in darkness be:
　　Compassionate, and merciful,
　　　and righteous, is he.

5　A good man doth his favour shew,
　　　and doth to others lend:
　　He with discretion his affairs
　　　will guide unto the end.
6　Surely there is not any thing
　　　that ever shall him move:

The righteous man's memorial
   shall everlasting prove.

7   When he shall evil tidings hear,
     he shall not be afraid:
   His heart is fix'd, his confidence
     upon the Lord is stay'd.
8   His heart is firmly stablished,
     afraid he shall not be,
   Until upon his enemies
     he his desire shall see.

9   He hath dispers'd, giv'n to the poor;
     his righteousness shall be
   To ages all; with honour shall
     his horn be raised high.
10 The wicked shall it see, and fret,
     his teeth gnash, melt away:
   What wicked men do most desire
     shall utterly decay.

Psalm 113

1   PRAISE God: ye servants of the Lord,
     O praise, the Lord's name praise.
2   Yea, blessed be the name of God
     from this time forth always.
3   From rising sun to where it sets,
     God's name is to be prais'd.
4   Above all nations God is high,
     'bove heav'ns his glory rais'd.

5   Unto the Lord our God that dwells
     on high, who can compare?

6   Himself that humbleth things to see
       in heav'n and earth that are.
7   He from the dust doth raise the poor,
       that very low doth lie;
    And from the dunghill lifts the man
       oppress'd with poverty;

8   That he may highly him advance,
       and with the princes set;
    With those that of his people are
       the chief, ev'n princes great.
9   The barren woman house to keep
       he maketh, and to be
    Of sons a mother full of joy.
       Praise to the Lord give ye.

Psalm 114

1   WHEN Isr'el out of Egypt went,
       and did his dwelling change,
    When Jacob's house went out from those
       that were of language strange,
2   He Judah did his sanctuary,
       his kingdom Isr'el make:
3   The sea it saw, and quickly fled,
       Jordan was driven back.

4   Like rams the mountains, and like lambs
       the hills skipp'd to and fro.
5   O sea, why fledd'st thou? Jordan, back
       why wast thou driven so?
6   Ye mountains great, wherefore was it
       that ye did skip like rams?
    And wherefore was it, little hills,
       that ye did leap like lambs?

7 O at the presence of the Lord,
   earth, tremble thou for fear,
While as the presence of the God
   of Jacob doth appear:

8 Who from the hard and stony rock
   did standing water bring;
And by his pow'r did turn the flint
   into a water-spring.

Psalm 115

1 NOT unto us, Lord, not to us,
   but do thou glory take
Unto thy name, ev'n for thy truth,
   and for thy mercy's sake.

2 O wherefore should the heathen say,
   Where is their God now gone?

3 But our God in the heavens is,
   what pleas'd him he hath done.

4 Their idols silver are and gold,
   work of men's hands they be.

5 Mouths have they, but they do not speak;
   and eyes, but do not see;

6 Ears have they, but they do not hear;
   noses, but savour not;

7 Hands, feet, but handle not, nor walk;
   nor speak they through their throat.

8 Like them their makers are, and all
   on them their trust that build.

9 O Isr'el, trust thou in the Lord,
   he is their help and shield.

10 O Aaron's house, trust in the Lord,
   their help and shield is he.

11 Ye that fear God, trust in the Lord,
    their help and shield he'll be.

12 The Lord of us hath mindful been,
    and he will bless us still:
He will the house of Isr'el bless,
    bless Aaron's house he will.

13 Both small and great, that fear the Lord,
    he will them surely bless.

14 The Lord will you, you and your seed,
    aye more and more increase.

15 O blessed are ye of the Lord,
    who made the earth and heav'n.

16 The heav'n, ev'n heav'ns, are God's, but he
    earth to men's sons hath giv'n.

17 The dead, nor who to silence go,
    God's praise do not record.

18 But henceforth we for ever will
    bless God. Praise ye the Lord.

Psalm 116

1 I LOVE the Lord, because my voice
    and prayers he did hear.

2 I, while I live, will call on him,
    who bow'd to me his ear.

3 Of death the cords and sorrows did
    about me compass round;
The pains of hell took hold on me,
    I grief and trouble found.

4 Upon the name of God the Lord
    then did I call, and say,

Deliver thou my soul, O Lord,
  I do thee humbly pray.
5 God merciful and righteous is,
  yea, gracious is our Lord.
6 God saves the meek: I was brought low,
  he did me help afford.

7 O thou my soul, do thou return
  unto thy quiet rest;
For largely, lo, the Lord to thee
  his bounty hath exprest.
8 For my distressed soul from death
  deliver'd was by thee:
Thou didst my mourning eyes from tears,
  my feet from falling, free.

9 I in the land of those that live
  will walk the Lord before.
10 I did believe, therefore I spake:
  I was afflicted sore.
11 I said, when I was in my haste,
  that all men liars be.
12 What shall I render to the Lord
  for all his gifts to me?

13 I'll of salvation take the cup,
  on God's name will I call:
14 I'll pay my vows now to the Lord
  before his people all.
15 Dear in God's sight is his saints' death.
16   Thy servant, Lord, am I;
Thy servant sure, thine handmaid's son:
  my bands thou didst untie.

17 Thank-off'rings I to thee will give,
    and on God's name will call.
18 I'll pay my vows now to the Lord
    before his people all;
19 Within the courts of God's own house,
    within the midst of thee,
O city of Jerusalem.
    Praise to the Lord give ye.

Psalm 117

1 O GIVE ye praise unto the Lord,
    all nations that be;
Likewise, ye people all, accord
    his name to magnify.
2 For great to us-ward ever are
    his loving-kindnesses:
His truth endures for evermore.
    The Lord O do ye bless.

Psalm 118

1 O PRAISE the Lord, for he is good;
    his mercy lasteth ever.
2 Let those of Israel now say,
    His mercy faileth never.
3 Now let the house of Aaron say,
    His mercy lasteth ever.
4 Let those that fear the Lord now say,
    His mercy faileth never.

5 I in distress call'd on the Lord;
    the Lord did answer me:
He in a large place did me set,
    from trouble made me free.

6 The mighty Lord is on my side,
    I will not be afraid;
For any thing that man can do
    I shall not be dismay'd.

7 The Lord doth take my part with them
    that help to succour me:
Therefore on those that do me hate
    I my desire shall see.

8 Better it is to trust in God
    than trust in man's defence;

9 Better to trust in God than make
    princes our confidence.

10 The nations, joining all in one,
    did compass me about:
But in the Lord's most holy name
    I shall them all root out.

11 They compass'd me about; I say,
    they compass'd me about:
But in the Lord's most holy name
    I shall them all root out.

12 Like bees they compass'd me about;
    like unto thorns that flame
They quenched are: for them shall I
    destroy in God's own name.

13 Thou sore hast thrust, that I might fall,
    but my Lord helped me.

14 God my salvation is become,
    my strength and song is he.

15 In dwellings of the righteous
    is heard the melody

Of joy and health: the Lord's right hand
    doth ever valiantly.
16 The right hand of the mighty Lord
    exalted is on high;
The right hand of the mighty Lord
    doth ever valiantly.

17 I shall not die, but live, and shall
    the works of God discover.
18 The Lord hath me chastised sore,
    but not to death giv'n over.
19 O set ye open unto me
    the gates of righteousness;
Then will I enter into them,
    and I the Lord will bless.

20 This is the gate of God, by it
    the just shall enter in.
21 Thee will I praise, for thou me heard'st
    and hast my safety been.
22 That stone is made head corner-stone,
    which builders did despise:
23 This is the doing of the Lord,
    and wondrous in our eyes.

24 This is the day God made, in it
    we'll joy triumphantly.
25 Save now, I pray thee, Lord; I pray,
    send now prosperity.
26 Blessed is he in God's great name
    that cometh us to save:
We, from the house which to the Lord
    pertains, you blessed have.

27 God is the Lord, who unto us
    hath made light to arise:
  Bind ye unto the altar's horns
    with cords the sacrifice.
28 Thou art my God, I'll thee exalt;
    my God, I will thee praise.
29 Give thanks to God, for he is good:
    his mercy lasts always.

Psalm 119

Aleph: The 1st Part.

1 BLESSED are they that undefil'd,
  and straight are in the way;
  Who in the Lord's most holy law
    do walk, and do not stray.
2 Blessed are they who to observe
    his statutes are inclin'd;
  And who do seek the living God
    with their whole heart and mind.

3 Such in his ways do walk, and they
    do no iniquity.
4 Thou hast commanded us to keep
    thy precepts carefully.
5 O that thy statutes to observe
    thou would'st my ways direct!
6 Then shall I not be sham'd, when I
    thy precepts all respect.

7 Then with integrity of heart
    thee will I praise and bless,
  When I the judgments all have learn'd
    of thy pure righteousness.

8 That I will keep thy statutes all
    firmly resolv'd have I:
    O do not then, most gracious God,
    forsake me utterly.

Beth: The 2nd Part.

9 By what means shall a young man learn
    his way to purify?
    If he according to thy word
    thereto attentive be.
10 Unfeignedly thee have I sought
    with all my soul and heart:
    O let me not from the right path
    of thy commands depart.

11 Thy word I in my heart have hid,
    that I offend not thee.
12 O Lord, thou ever blessed art,
    thy statutes teach thou me.
13 The judgments of thy mouth each one
    my lips declared have:
14 More joy thy testimonies' way
    than riches all me gave.

15 I will thy holy precepts make
    my meditation;
    And carefully I'll have respect
    unto thy ways each one.
16 Upon thy statutes my delight
    shall constantly be set:
    And, by thy grace, I never will
    thy holy word forget.

Gimel: The 3rd Part.

17 With me thy servant, in thy grace,
    deal bountifully, Lord;
  That by thy favour I may live,
    and duly keep thy word.
18 Open mine eyes, that of thy law
    the wonders I may see.
19 I am a stranger on this earth,
    hide not thy laws from me.

20 My soul within me breaks, and doth
    much fainting still endure,
  Through longing that it hath all times
    unto thy judgments pure.
21 Thou hast rebuk'd the cursed proud,
    who from thy precepts swerve.
22 Reproach and shame remove from me,
    for I thy laws observe.

23 Against me princes spake with spite,
    while they in council sat:
  But I thy servant did upon
    thy statutes meditate.
24 My comfort, and my heart's delight,
    thy testimonies be;
  And they, in all my doubts and fears,
    are counsellors to me.

Daleth: The 4th Part.

25 My soul to dust cleaves: quicken me,
    according to thy word.
26 My ways I shew'd, and me thou heard'st:
    teach me thy statutes, Lord.

27 The way of thy commandements
    make me aright to know;
So all thy works that wondrous are
    I shall to others show.

28 My soul doth melt, and drop away,
    for heaviness and grief:
To me, according to thy word,
    give strength, and send relief.

29 From me the wicked way of lies
    let far removed be;
And graciously thy holy law
    do thou grant unto me.

30 I chosen have the perfect way
    of truth and verity:
Thy judgments that most righteous are
    before me laid have I.

31 I to thy testimonies cleave;
    shame do not on me cast.

32 I'll run thy precepts' way, when thou
    my heart enlarged hast.

He: The 5th Part.

33 Teach me, O Lord, the perfect way
    of thy precepts divine,
And to observe it to the end
    I shall my heart incline.

34 Give understanding unto me,
    so keep thy law shall I;
Yea, ev'n with my whole heart I shall
    observe it carefully.

35 In thy law's path make me to go;
    for I delight therein.

36 My heart unto thy testimonies,
     and not to greed, incline.
37 Turn thou away my sight and eyes
     from viewing vanity;
   And in thy good and holy way
     be pleas'd to quicken me.

38 Confirm to me thy gracious word,
     which I did gladly hear,
   Ev'n to thy servant, Lord, who is
     devoted to thy fear.
39 Turn thou away my fear'd reproach;
     for good thy judgments be.
40 Lo, for thy precepts I have long'd;
     in thy truth quicken me.

Vau: The 6th Part.

41 Let thy sweet mercies also come
     and visit me, O Lord;
   Ev'n thy benign salvation,
     according to thy word.
42 So shall I have wherewith I may
     give him an answer just,
   Who spitefully reproacheth me;
     for in thy word I trust.

43 The word of truth out of my mouth
     take thou not utterly;
   For on thy judgments righteous
     my hope doth still rely.
44 So shall I keep for evermore
     thy law continually.
45 And, sith that I thy precepts seek,
     I'll walk at liberty.

46 I'll speak thy word to kings, and I
    with shame shall not be mov'd;
47 And will delight myself always
    in thy laws, which I lov'd.
48 To thy commandments, which I lov'd,
    my hands lift up I will;
  And I will also meditate
    upon thy statutes still.

Zain: The 7th Part.

49 Remember, Lord, thy gracious word
    thou to thy servant spake,
  Which, for a ground of my sure hope,
    thou causedst me to take.
50 This word of thine my comfort is
    in mine affliction:
  For in my straits I am reviv'd
    by this thy word alone.

51 The men whose hearts with pride are
        stuff'd
    did greatly me deride;
  Yet from thy straight commandements
    I have not turn'd aside.
52 Thy judgments righteous, O Lord,
    which thou of old forth gave,
  I did remember, and myself
    by them comforted have.

53 Horror took hold on me, because
    ill men thy law forsake.
54 I in my house of pilgrimage
    thy laws my songs do make.

55 Thy name by night, Lord, I did mind,
    and I have kept thy law.
56 And this I had, because thy word
    I kept, and stood in awe.

Cheth: The 8th Part.

57 Thou my sure portion art alone,
    which I did chuse, O Lord:
  I have resolv'd, and said, that I
    would keep thy holy word.
58 With my whole heart I did entreat
    thy face and favour free:
  According to thy gracious word
    be merciful to me.

59 I thought upon my former ways,
    and did my life well try;
  And to thy testimonies pure
    my feet then turned I.
60 I did not stay, nor linger long,
    as those that slothful are;
  But hastily thy laws to keep
    myself I did prepare.

61 Bands of ill men me robb'd; yet I
    thy precepts did not slight.
62 I'll rise at midnight thee to praise,
    ev'n for thy judgments right.
63 I am companion to all those
    who fear, and thee obey.
64 O Lord, thy mercy fills the earth:
    teach me thy laws, I pray.

Teth: The 9th Part.

65 Well hast thou with thy servant dealt,
   as thou didst promise give.
66 Good judgment me, and knowledge teach,
   for I thy word believe.
67 Ere I afflicted was I stray'd;
   but now I keep thy word.
68 Both good thou art, and good thou do'st:
   teach me thy statutes, Lord.

69 The men that are puff'd up with pride
   against me forg'd a lie;
   Yet thy commandements observe
   with my whole heart will I.
70 Their hearts, through worldly ease and
                 wealth,
   as fat as grease they be:
   But in thy holy law I take
   delight continually.

71 It hath been very good for me
   that I afflicted was,
   That I might well instructed be,
   and learn thy holy laws.
72 The word that cometh from thy mouth
   is better unto me
   Than many thousands and great sums
   of gold and silver be.

Jod: The 10th Part.

73 Thou mad'st and fashion'dst me: thy laws
   to know give wisdom, Lord.
74 So who thee fear shall joy to see
   me trusting in thy word.

75 That very right thy judgments are
    I know, and do confess;
And that thou hast afflicted me
    in truth and faithfulness.

76 O let thy kindness merciful,
    I pray thee, comfort me,
As to thy servant faithfully
    was promised by thee.
77 And let thy tender mercies come
    to me, that I may live;
Because thy holy laws to me
    sweet delectation give.

78 Lord, let the proud ashamed be;
    for they, without a cause,
With me perversely dealt: but I
    will muse upon thy laws.
79 Let such as fear thee, and have known
    thy statutes, turn to me.
80 My heart let in thy laws be sound,
    that sham'd I never be.

Caph: The 11th Part.

81 My soul for thy salvation faints;
    yet I thy word believe.
82 Mine eyes fail for thy word: I say,
    When wilt thou comfort give?
83 For like a bottle I'm become,
    that in the smoke is set:
I'm black, and parch'd with grief; yet I
    thy statutes not forget.

84 How many are thy servant's days?
    when wilt thou execute

> Just judgment on these wicked men
>   that do me persecute?

85 The proud have digged pits for me,
    which is against thy laws.
86 Thy words all faithful are: help me,
    pursu'd without a cause.

87 They so consum'd me, that on earth
    my life they scarce did leave:
  Thy precepts yet forsook I not,
    but close to them did cleave.
88 After thy loving-kindness, Lord,
    me quicken, and preserve:
  The testimony of thy mouth
    so shall I still observe.

Lamed: The 12th Part.

89 Thy word for ever is, O Lord,
    in heaven settled fast;
90 Unto all generations
    thy faithfulness doth last:
  The earth thou hast established,
    and it abides by thee.
91 This day they stand as thou ordain'dst;
    for all thy servants be.

92 Unless in thy most perfect law
    my soul delights had found,
  I should have perished, when as
    my troubles did abound.
93 Thy precepts I will ne'er forget;
    they quick'ning to me brought.
94 Lord, I am thine; O save thou me:
    thy precepts I have sought.

95 For me the wicked have laid wait,
    me seeking to destroy:
But I thy testimonies true
    consider will with joy.
96 An end of all perfection
    here have I seen, O God:
But as for thy commandement,
    it is exceeding broad.

Mem: The 13th Part.

97 O how love I thy law! it is
    my study all the day:
98 It makes me wiser than my foes;
    for it doth with me stay.
99 Than all my teachers now I have
    more understanding far;
Because my meditation
    thy testimonies are.

100 In understanding I excel
    those that are ancients;
For I endeavoured to keep
    all thy commandements.
101 My feet from each ill way I stay'd,
    that I may keep thy word.
102 I from thy judgments have not swerv'd;
    for thou hast taught me, Lord.

103 How sweet unto my taste, O Lord,
    are all thy words of truth!
Yea, I do find them sweeter far
    than honey to my mouth.
104 I through thy precepts, that are pure,
    do understanding get;

I therefore ev'ry way that's false
with all my heart do hate.

Nun: The 14th Part.

105 Thy word is to my feet a lamp,
and to my path a light.
106 I sworn have, and I will perform,
to keep thy judgments right.
107 I am with sore affliction
ev'n overwhelm'd, O Lord:
In mercy raise and quicken me,
according to thy word.

108 The free-will-off'rings of my mouth
accept, I thee beseech:
And unto me thy servant, Lord,
thy judgments clearly teach.
109 Though still my soul be in my hand,
thy laws I'll not forget.
110 I err'd not from them, though for me
the wicked snares did set.

111 I of thy testimonies have
above all things made choice,
To be my heritage for aye;
for they my heart rejoice.
112 I carefully inclined have
my heart still to attend;
That I thy statutes may perform
alway unto the end.

Samech: The 15th Part.

113 I hate the thoughts of vanity,
but love thy law do I.

114 My shield and hiding-place thou art:
    I on thy word rely.
115 All ye that evil-doers are
    from me depart away;
    For the commandments of my God
    I purpose to obey.

116 According to thy faithful word
    uphold and stablish me,
    That I may live, and of my hope
    ashamed never be.
117 Hold thou me up, so shall I be
    in peace and safety still;
    And to thy statutes have respect
    continually I will.

118 Thou tread'st down all that love to stray;
    false their deceit doth prove.
119 Lewd men, like dross, away thou putt'st;
    therefore thy law I love.
120 For fear of thee my very flesh
    doth tremble, all dismay'd;
    And of thy righteous judgments, Lord,
    my soul is much afraid.

Ain: The 16th Part.

121 To all men I have judgment done,
    performing justice right;
    Then let me not be left unto
    my fierce oppressors' might.
122 For good unto thy servant, Lord,
    thy servant's surety be:
    From the oppression of the proud
    do thou deliver me.

123 Mine eyes do fail with looking long
    for thy salvation,
  The word of thy pure righteousness
    while I do wait upon.
124 In mercy with thy servant deal,
    thy laws me teach and show.
125 I am thy servant, wisdom give,
    that I thy laws may know.

126 'Tis time thou work, Lord; for they have
    made void thy law divine.
127 Therefore thy precepts more I love
    than gold, yea, gold most fine.
128 Concerning all things thy commands
    all right I judge therefore;
  And ev'ry false and wicked way
    I perfectly abhor.

Pe: The 17th Part.

129 Thy statutes, Lord, are wonderful,
    my soul them keeps with care.
130 The entrance of thy words gives light,
    makes wise who simple are.
131 My mouth I have wide opened,
    and panted earnestly,
  While after thy commandements
    I long'd exceedingly.

132 Look on me, Lord, and merciful
    do thou unto me prove,
  As thou art wont to do to those
    thy name who truly love.
133 O let my footsteps in thy word
    aright still order'd be:

Let no iniquity obtain
dominion over me.

134 From man's oppression save thou me;
so keep thy laws I will.
135 Thy face make on thy servant shine;
teach me thy statutes still.
136 Rivers of waters from mine eyes
did run down, when I saw
How wicked men run on in sin,
and do not keep thy law.

Tsaddi: The 18th Part.

137 O Lord, thou art most righteous;
thy judgments are upright.
138 Thy testimonies thou command'st
most faithful are and right.
139 My zeal hath ev'n consumed me,
because mine enemies
Thy holy words forgotten have,
and do thy laws despise.

140 Thy word's most pure, therefore on it
thy servant's love is set.
141 Small, and despis'd I am, yet I
thy precepts not forget.
142 Thy righteousness is righteousness
which ever doth endure:
Thy holy law, Lord, also is
the very truth most pure.

143 Trouble and anguish have me found,
and taken hold on me:

Yet in my trouble my delight
thy just commandments be.
144 Eternal righteousness is in
thy testimonies all:
Lord, to me understanding give,
and ever live I shall.

Qoph: The 19th Part.

145 With my whole heart I cry'd, Lord, hear;
I will thy word obey.
146 I cry'd to thee; save me, and I
will keep thy laws alway.
147 I of the morning did prevent
the dawning, and did cry:
For all mine expectation
did on thy word rely.

148 Mine eyes did timeously prevent
the watches of the night,
That in thy word with careful mind
then meditate I might.
149 After thy loving-kindness hear
my voice, that calls on thee:
According to thy judgment, Lord,
revive and quicken me.

150 Who follow mischief they draw nigh;
they from thy law are far:
151 But thou art near, Lord; most firm truth
all thy commandments are.
152 As for thy testimonies all,
of old this have I try'd,
That thou hast surely founded them
for ever to abide.

153 Consider mine affliction,
    in safety do me set:
  Deliver me, O Lord, for I
    thy law do not forget.
154 After thy word revive thou me:
    save me, and plead my cause.
155 Salvation is from sinners far;
    for they seek not thy laws.

156 O Lord, both great and manifold
    thy tender mercies be:
  According to thy judgments just,
    revive and quicken me.
157 My persecutors many are,
    and foes that do combine;
  Yet from thy testimonies pure
    my heart doth not decline.

158 I saw transgressors, and was griev'd;
    for they keep not thy word.
159 See how I love thy law! as thou
    art kind, me quicken, Lord.
160 From the beginning all thy word
    hath been most true and sure:
  Thy righteous judgments ev'ry one
    for evermore endure.

161 Princes have persecuted me,
    although no cause they saw:
  But still of thy most holy word
    my heart doth stand in awe.

162 I at thy word rejoice, as one
 of spoil that finds great store.
163 Thy law I love; but lying all
 I hate and do abhor.

164 Sev'n times a-day it is my care
 to give due praise to thee;
 Because of all thy judgments, Lord,
 which righteous ever be.
165 Great peace have they who love thy law;
 offence they shall have none.
166 I hop'd for thy salvation, Lord,
 and thy commands have done.

167 My soul thy testimonies pure
 observed carefully;
 On them my heart is set, and them
 I love exceedingly.
168 Thy testimonies and thy laws
 I kept with special care;
 For all my works and ways each one
 before thee open are.

Tau: The 22nd Part.

169 O let my earnest pray'r and cry
 come near before thee, Lord:
 Give understanding unto me,
 according to thy word.
170 Let my request before thee come:
 after thy word me free.
171 My lips shall utter praise, when thou
 hast taught thy laws to me.

172 My tongue of thy most blessed word
 shall speak, and it confess;

Because all thy commandements
    are perfect righteousness.
173 Let thy strong hand make help to me:
    thy precepts are my choice.
174 I long'd for thy salvation, Lord,
    and in thy law rejoice.

175 O let my soul live, and it shall
    give praises unto thee;
    And let thy judgments gracious
    be helpful unto me.
176 I, like a lost sheep, went astray;
    thy servant seek, and find:
    For thy commands I suffer'd not
    to slip out of my mind.

Psalm 120

A Song of degrees.

1   IN my distress to God I cry'd,
    and he gave ear to me.
2   From lying lips, and guileful tongue,
    O Lord, my soul set free.
3   What shall be giv'n thee? or what shall
    be done to thee, false tongue?
4   Ev'n burning coals of juniper,
    sharp arrows of the strong.

5   Woe's me that I in Mesech am
    a sojourner so long;
    That I in tabernacles dwell
    to Kedar that belong.
6   My soul with him that hateth peace
    hath long a dweller been.

7   I am for peace; but when I speak,
         for battle they are keen.

Psalm 121

A Song of degrees.

1   I TO the hills will lift mine eyes,
         from whence doth come mine aid.
2   My safety cometh from the Lord,
         who heav'n and earth hath made.
3   Thy foot he'll not let slide, nor will
         he slumber that thee keeps.
4   Behold, he that keeps Israel,
         he slumbers not, nor sleeps.

5   The Lord thee keeps, the Lord thy shade
         on thy right hand doth stay:
6   The moon by night thee shall not smite,
         nor yet the sun by day.
7   The Lord shall keep thy soul; he shall
         preserve thee from all ill.
8   Henceforth thy going out and in
         God keep for ever will.

Psalm 122

A Song of degrees of David.

1   I JOY'D when to the house of God,
         Go up, they said to me.
2   Jerusalem, within thy gates
         our feet shall standing be.
3   Jerus'lem, as a city, is
         compactly built together:
4   Unto that place the tribes go up,
         the tribes of God go thither:

To Isr'el's testimony, there
to God's name thanks to pay.
5 For thrones of judgment, ev'n the thrones
of David's house, there stay.
6 Pray that Jerusalem may have
peace and felicity:
Let them that love thee and thy peace
have still prosperity.

7 Therefore I wish that peace may still
within thy walls remain,
And ever may thy palaces
prosperity retain.
8 Now, for my friends' and brethren's sakes,
Peace be in thee, I'll say.
9 And for the house of God our Lord,
I'll seek thy good alway.

Psalm 123

A Song of degrees.

1 O THOU that dwellest in the heav'ns,
I lift mine eyes to thee.
2 Behold, as servants' eyes do look
their masters' hand to see,
As handmaid's eyes her mistress' hand;
so do our eyes attend
Upon the Lord our God, until
to us he mercy send.

3 O Lord, be gracious to us,
unto us gracious be;
Because replenish'd with contempt
exceedingly are we.

4 Our soul is fill'd with scorn of those
 that at their ease abide,
And with the insolent contempt
 of those that swell in pride.

Psalm 124

A Song of degrees of David.

1 HAD not the Lord been on our side,
 may Israel now say;
2 Had not the Lord been on our side,
 when men rose us to slay;
3 They had us swallow'd quick, when as
 their wrath 'gainst us did flame:
4 Waters had cover'd us, our soul
 had sunk beneath the stream.

5 Then had the waters, swelling high,
 over our soul made way.
6 Bless'd be the Lord, who to their teeth
 us gave not for a prey.
7 Our soul's escaped, as a bird
 out of the fowler's snare;
The snare asunder broken is,
 and we escaped are.

8 Our sure and all-sufficient help
 is in JEHOVAH's name;
His name who did the heav'n create,
 and who the earth did frame.

Another of the same

1 NOW Israel
 may say, and that truly,

If that the Lord
   had not our cause maintain'd;
2 If that the Lord
   had not our right sustain'd,
When cruel men
   against us furiously
Rose up in wrath,
   to make of us their prey;

3 Then certainly
   they had devour'd us all,
And swallow'd quick,
   for ought that we could deem;
Such was their rage,
   as we might well esteem.
4 And as fierce floods
   before them all things drown,
So had they brought
   our soul to death quite down.

5 The raging streams,
   with their proud swelling waves,
Had then our soul
   o'erwhelmed in the deep.
6 But bless'd be God,
   who doth us safely keep,
And hath not giv'n
   us for a living prey
Unto their teeth,
   and bloody cruelty.

7 Ev'n as a bird
   out of the fowler's snare
Escapes away,
   so is our soul set free:

Broke are their nets,
   and thus escaped we.
8 Therefore our help
   is in the Lord's great name,
Who heav'n and earth
   by his great pow'r did frame.

Psalm 125

A Song of degrees.

1 THEY in the Lord that firmly trust
   shall be like Sion hill,
Which at no time can be remov'd,
   but standeth ever still.
2 As round about Jerusalem
   the mountains stand alway,
The Lord his folk doth compass so,
   from henceforth and for aye.

3 For ill men's rod upon the lot
   of just men shall not lie;
Lest righteous men stretch forth their hands
   unto iniquity.
4 Do thou to all those that be good
   thy goodness, Lord, impart;
And do thou good to those that are
   upright within their heart.

5 But as for such as turn aside
   after their crooked way,
God shall lead forth with wicked men:
   on Isr'el peace shall stay.

Psalm 126

A Song of degrees.

1 WHEN Sion's bondage God turn'd back,
    as men that dream'd were we.
2 Then fill'd with laughter was our mouth,
    our tongue with melody:
They 'mong the heathen said, The Lord
    great things for them hath wrought.
3 The Lord hath done great things for us,
    whence joy to us is brought.

4 As streams of water in the south,
    our bondage, Lord, recall.
5 Who sow in tears, a reaping time
    of joy enjoy they shall.
6 That man who, bearing precious seed,
    in going forth doth mourn,
He doubtless, bringing back his sheaves,
    rejoicing shall return.

Psalm 127

A Song of degrees for Solomon.

1 EXCEPT the Lord do build the house,
    the builders lose their pain:
Except the Lord the city keep,
    the watchmen watch in vain.
2 'Tis vain for you to rise betimes,
    or late from rest to keep,
To feed on sorrows' bread; so gives
    he his beloved sleep.

3 Lo, children are God's heritage,
    the womb's fruit his reward.

4 The sons of youth as arrows are,
    for strong men's hands prepar'd.
5 O happy is the man that hath
    his quiver fill'd with those;
They unashamed in the gate
    shall speak unto their foes.

Psalm 128

A Song of degrees.

1 **B**LESS'D is each one that fears the Lord,
    and walketh in his ways;
2 For of thy labour thou shalt eat,
    and happy be always.
3 Thy wife shall as a fruitful vine
    by thy house' sides be found:
Thy children like to olive-plants
    about thy table round.

4 Behold, the man that fears the Lord,
    thus blessed shall he be.
5 The Lord shall out of Sion give
    his blessing unto thee:
Thou shalt Jerus'lem's good behold
    whilst thou on earth dost dwell.
6 Thou shalt thy children's children see,
    and peace on Israel.

Psalm 129

A Song of degrees.

1 **O**FT did they vex me from my youth,
    may Isr'el now declare;
2 Oft did they vex me from my youth,
    yet not victorious were.

3 The plowers plow'd upon my back;
    they long their furrows drew.
4 The righteous Lord did cut the cords
    of the ungodly crew.

5 Let Sion's haters all be turn'd
    back with confusion.
6 As grass on houses' tops be they,
    which fades ere it be grown:
7 Whereof enough to fill his hand
    the mower cannot find;
Nor can the man his bosom fill,
    whose work is sheaves to bind.

8 Neither say they who do go by,
    God's blessing on you rest:
We in the name of God the Lord
    do wish you to be blest.

Psalm 130

A Song of degrees.

1 LORD, from the depths to thee I cry'd.
2   My voice, Lord, do thou hear:
Unto my supplication's voice
    give an attentive ear.
3 Lord, who shall stand, if thou, O Lord,
    should'st mark iniquity?
4 But yet with thee forgiveness is,
    that fear'd thou mayest be.

5 I wait for God, my soul doth wait,
    my hope is in his word.
6 More than they that for morning watch,
    my soul waits for the Lord;

I say, more than they that do watch
the morning light to see.
7 Let Israel hope in the Lord,
for with him mercies be;

And plenteous redemption
is ever found with him.
8 And from all his iniquities
he Isr'el shall redeem.

Psalm *131*

A Song of degrees of David.

1 MY heart not haughty is, O Lord,
mine eyes not lofty be;
Nor do I deal in matters great,
or things too high for me.
2 I surely have myself behav'd
with quiet sp'rit and mild,
As child of mother wean'd: my soul
is like a weaned child.

3 Upon the Lord let all the hope
of Israel rely,
Ev'n from the time that present is
unto eternity.

Psalm *132*

A Song of degrees.

1 DAVID, and his afflictions all,
Lord, do thou think upon;
2 How unto God he sware, and vow'd
to Jacob's mighty One.
3 I will not come within my house,
nor rest in bed at all;

4   Nor shall mine eyes take any sleep,
        nor eyelids slumber shall;

5   Till for the Lord a place I find,
        where he may make abode;
     A place of habitation
        for Jacob's mighty God.
6   Lo, at the place of Ephratah
        of it we understood;
     And we did find it in the fields,
        and city of the wood.

7   We'll go into his tabernacles,
        and at his footstool bow.
8   Arise, O Lord, into thy rest,
        th' ark of thy strength, and thou.
9   O let thy priests be clothed, Lord,
        with truth and righteousness;
     And let all those that are thy saints
        shout loud for joyfulness.

10   For thine own servant David's sake,
        do not deny thy grace;
     Nor of thine own anointed one
        turn thou away the face.
11   The Lord in truth to David sware,
        he will not turn from it,
     I of thy body's fruit will make
        upon thy throne to sit.

12   My cov'nant if thy sons will keep,
        and laws to them made known,
     Their children then shall also sit
        for ever on thy throne.

13 For God of Sion hath made choice;
    there he desires to dwell.
14 This is my rest, here still I'll stay;
    for I do like it well.

15 Her food I'll greatly bless; her poor
    with bread will satisfy.
16 Her priests I'll clothe with health; her saints
    shall shout forth joyfully.
17 And there will I make David's horn
    to bud forth pleasantly:
For him that mine anointed is
    a lamp ordain'd have I.

18 As with a garment I will clothe
    with shame his en'mies all:
But yet the crown that he doth wear
    upon him flourish shall.

Psalm 133

A Song of degrees of David.

1 BEHOLD, how good a thing it is,
    and how becoming well,
Together such as brethren are
    in unity to dwell!
2 Like precious ointment on the head,
    that down the beard did flow,
Ev'n Aaron's beard, and to the skirts
    did of his garments go.

3 As Hermon's dew, the dew that doth
    on Sion' hills descend:
For there the blessing God commands,
    life that shall never end.

Psalm 134

A Song of degrees.

1 BEHOLD, bless ye the Lord, all ye
that his attendants are,
Ev'n you that in God's temple be,
  and praise him nightly there.
2 Your hands within God's holy place
  lift up, and praise his name.
3 From Sion' hill the Lord thee bless,
  that heav'n and earth did frame.

Psalm 135

1 PRAISE ye the Lord, the Lord's name
  praise;
his servants, praise ye God.
2 Who stand in God's house, in the courts
  of our God make abode.
3 Praise ye the Lord, for he is good;
  unto him praises sing:
Sing praises to his name, because
  it is a pleasant thing.

4 For Jacob to himself the Lord
  did chuse of his good pleasure,
And he hath chosen Israel
  for his peculiar treasure.
5 Because I know assuredly
  the Lord is very great,
And that our Lord above all gods
  in glory hath his seat.

6 What things soever pleas'd the Lord,
  that in the heav'n did he,

And in the earth, the seas, and all
    the places deep that be.
7 He from the ends of earth doth make
    the vapours to ascend;
With rain he lightnings makes, and wind
    doth from his treasures send.

8 Egypt's first-born, from man to beast
9   who smote. Strange tokens he
On Phar'oh and his servants sent,
    Egypt, in midst of thee.
10 He smote great nations, slew great kings:
11   Sihon of Heshbon king,
And Og of Bashan, and to nought
    did Canaan's kingdoms bring:

12 And for a wealthy heritage
    their pleasant land he gave,
An heritage which Israel,
    his chosen folk, should have.
13 Thy name, O Lord, shall still endure,
    and thy memorial
With honour shall continu'd be
    to generations all.

14 For why? the righteous God will judge
    his people righteously;
Concerning those that do him serve,
    himself repent will he.
15 The idols of the nations
    of silver are and gold,
And by the hands of men is made
    their fashion and mould.

16 Mouths have they, but they do not speak;
    eyes, but they do not see;
17 Ears have they, but hear not; and in
    their mouths no breathing be.
18 Their makers are like them; so are
    all that on them rely.
19 O Isr'el's house, bless God; bless God,
    O Aaron's family.

20 O bless the Lord, of Levi's house
    ye who his servants are;
And bless the holy name of God,
    all ye the Lord that fear.
21 And blessed be the Lord our God
    from Sion's holy hill,
Who dwelleth at Jerusalem.
    The Lord O praise ye still.

Psalm 136

1 GIVE thanks to God, for good is he:
    for mercy hath he ever.
2 Thanks to the God of gods give ye:
    for his grace faileth never.
3 Thanks give the Lord of lords unto:
    for mercy hath he ever.
4 Who only wonders great can do:
    for his grace faileth never.

5 Who by his wisdom made heav'ns high:
    for mercy hath he ever.
6 Who stretch'd the earth above the sea:
    for his grace faileth never.
7 To him that made the great lights shine:
    for mercy hath he ever.

8   The sun to rule till day decline:
      for his grace faileth never.

9   The moon and stars to rule by night:
      for mercy hath he ever.

10 Who Egypt's first-born kill'd outright:
      for his grace faileth never.

11 And Isr'el brought from Egypt land:
      for mercy hath he ever.

12 With stretch'd-out arm, and with strong
          hand:
      for his grace faileth never.

13 By whom the Red sea parted was:
      for mercy hath he ever.

14 And through its midst made Isr'el pass:
      for his grace faileth never.

15 But Phar'oh and his host did drown:
      for mercy hath he ever.

16 Who through the desert led his own:
      for his grace faileth never.

17 To him great kings who overthrew:
      for he hath mercy ever.

18 Yea, famous kings in battle slew:
      for his grace faileth never.

19 Ev'n Sihon king of Amorites:
      for he hath mercy ever.

20 And Og the king of Bashanites:
      for his grace faileth never.

21 Their land in heritage to have:
      for mercy hath he ever.

22 His servant Isr'el right he gave:
   for his grace faileth never.
23 In our low state who on us thought:
   for he hath mercy ever.
24 And from our foes our freedom wrought:
   for his grace faileth never.

25 Who doth all flesh with food relieve:
   for he hath mercy ever.
26 Thanks to the God of heaven give:
   for his grace faileth never.

Another of the same

1 PRAISE God, for he is kind:
   His mercy lasts for aye.
2 Give thanks with heart and mind
   To God of gods alway:
      For certainly
      His mercies dure
      Most firm and sure
      Eternally.

3 The Lord of lords praise ye,
   Whose mercies still endure.
4 Great wonders only he
   Doth work by his great pow'r
      For certainly
      His mercies dure
      Most firm and sure
      Eternally.

5 Which God omnipotent,
   By might and wisdom high,
   The heav'n and firmament
   Did frame, as we may see:

> For certainly
> His mercies dure
> Most firm and sure
> Eternally.

6   To him who did outstretch
    This earth so great and wide,
    Above the waters' reach
    Making it to abide:
    >   For certainly
    >   His mercies dure
    >   Most firm and sure
    >   Eternally.

7   Great lights he made to be;
    For his grace lasteth aye:
8   Such as the sun we see,
    To rule the lightsome day:
    >   For certainly
    >   His mercies dure
    >   Most firm and sure
    >   Eternally.

9   Also the moon so clear,
    Which shineth in our sight;
    The stars that do appear,
    To guide the darksome night:
    >   For certainly
    >   His mercies dure
    >   Most firm and sure
    >   Eternally.

10 To him that Egypt smote,
    Who did his message scorn;

And in his anger hot
Did kill all their first-born:
   For certainly
   His mercies dure
   Most firm and sure
   Eternally.

11 Thence Isr'el out he brought;
    For his grace lasteth ever.
12 With a strong hand he wrought,
    And stretch'd-out arm deliver:
   For certainly
   His mercies dure
   Most firm and sure
   Eternally.

13 The sea he cut in two;
    For his grace lasteth still.
14 And through its midst to go
    Made his own Israel:
   For certainly
   His mercies dure
   Most firm and sure
   Eternally.

15 But overwhelm'd and lost
    Was proud king Pharaoh,
    With all his mighty host,
    And chariots there also:
   For certainly
   His mercies dure
   Most firm and sure
   Eternally.

16 To him who pow'rfully
His chosen people led,
Ev'n through the desert dry,
And in that place them fed:
 For certainly
 His mercies dure
 Most firm and sure
 Eternally.

17 To him great kings who smote;
For his grace hath no bound.
18 Who slew, and spared not
Kings famous and renown'd:
 For certainly
 His mercies dure
 Most firm and sure
 Eternally.

19 Sihon the Am'rites' king;
For his grace lasteth ever:
20 Og also, who did reign
The land of Bashan over:
 For certainly
 His mercies dure
 Most firm and sure
 Eternally.

21 Their land by lot he gave;
For his grace faileth never,
22 That Isr'el might it have
In heritage for ever:
 For certainly
 His mercies dure
 Most firm and sure
 Eternally.

23 Who hath remembered
   Us in our low estate;
24 And us delivered
   From foes which did us hate:
      For certainly
      His mercies dure
      Most firm and sure
      Eternally.

25 Who to all flesh gives food;
   For his grace faileth never.
26 Give thanks to God most good,
   The God of heav'n, for ever:
      For certainly
      His mercies dure
      Most firm and sure
      Eternally.

Psalm 137

1 **B**Y Babel's streams we sat and wept,
   when Sion we thought on.
2 In midst thereof we hang'd our harps
   the willow-trees upon.
3 For there a song required they,
   who did us captive bring:
   Our spoilers call'd for mirth, and said,
   A song of Sion sing.

4 O how the Lord's song shall we sing
   within a foreign land?
5 If thee, Jerus'lem, I forget,
   skill part from my right hand.
6 My tongue to my mouth's roof let cleave,
   if I do thee forget,

Jerusalem, and thee above
  my chief joy do not set.

7 Remember Edom's children, Lord,
    who in Jerus'lem's day,
  Ev'n unto its foundation,
    Raze, raze it quite, did say.
8 O daughter thou of Babylon,
    near to destruction;
  Bless'd shall he be that thee rewards,
    as thou to us hast done.

9 Yea, happy surely shall he be
    thy tender little ones
  Who shall lay hold upon, and them
    shall dash against the stones.

Psalm 138

A Psalm of David.

1 THEE will I praise with all my heart,
    I will sing praise to thee
2 Before the gods: And worship will
    toward thy sanctuary.
  I'll praise thy name, ev'n for thy truth,
    and kindness of thy love;
  For thou thy word hast magnify'd
    all thy great name above.

3 Thou didst me answer in the day
    when I to thee did cry;
  And thou my fainting soul with strength
    didst strengthen inwardly.
4 All kings upon the earth that are
    shall give thee praise, O Lord;

When as they from thy mouth shall hear
   thy true and faithful word.

5 Yea, in the righteous ways of God
   with gladness they shall sing:
For great's the glory of the Lord,
   who doth for ever reign.
6 Though God be high, yet he respects
   all those that lowly be;
Whereas the proud and lofty ones
   afar off knoweth he.

7 Though I in midst of trouble walk,
   I life from thee shall have:
'Gainst my foes' wrath thou'lt stretch thine
     hand;
   thy right hand shall me save.
8 Surely that which concerneth me
   the Lord will perfect make:
Lord, still thy mercy lasts; do not
   thine own hands' works forsake.

Psalm 139

To the chief Musician, A Psalm of David.

1 O LORD, thou hast me search'd and
      known.
2   Thou know'st my sitting down,
And rising up; yea, all my thoughts
   afar to thee are known.
3 My footsteps, and my lying down,
   thou compassest always;
Thou also most entirely art
   acquaint with all my ways.

4 For in my tongue, before I speak,
    not any word can be,
But altogether, lo, O Lord,
    it is well known to thee.
5 Behind, before, thou hast beset,
    and laid on me thine hand.
6 Such knowledge is too strange for me,
    too high to understand.

7 From thy Sp'rit whither shall I go?
    or from thy presence fly?
8 Ascend I heav'n, lo, thou art there;
    there, if in hell I lie.
9 Take I the morning wings, and dwell
    in utmost parts of sea;
10 Ev'n there, Lord, shall thy hand me lead,
    thy right hand hold shall me.

11 If I do say that darkness shall
    me cover from thy sight,
Then surely shall the very night
    about me be as light.
12 Yea, darkness hideth not from thee,
    but night doth shine as day:
To thee the darkness and the light
    are both alike alway.

13 For thou possessed hast my reins,
    and thou hast cover'd me,
When I within my mother's womb
    inclosed was by thee.
14 Thee will I praise; for fearfully
    and strangely made I am;

Thy works are marv'llous, and right well
  my soul doth know the same.

15 My substance was not hid from thee,
    when as in secret I
  Was made; and in earth's lowest parts
    was wrought most curiously.
16 Thine eyes my substance did behold,
    yet being unperfect;
  And in the volume of thy book
    my members all were writ;

  Which after in continuance
    were fashion'd ev'ry one,
  When as they yet all shapeless were,
    and of them there was none.
17 How precious also are thy thoughts,
    O gracious God, to me!
  And in their sum how passing great
    and numberless they be!

18 If I should count them, than the sand
    they more in number be:
  What time soever I awake,
    I ever am with thee.
19 Thou, Lord, wilt sure the wicked slay:
    hence from me bloody men.
20 Thy foes against thee loudly speak,
    and take thy name in vain.

21 Do not I hate all those, O Lord,
    that hatred bear to thee?
  With those that up against thee rise
    can I but grieved be?

22 With perfect hatred them I hate,
    my foes I them do hold.
23 Search me, O God, and know my heart,
    try me, my thoughts unfold:

24 And see if any wicked way
    there be at all in me;
  And in thine everlasting way
    to me a leader be.

Psalm 140

To the chief Musician, A Psalm of David.

1 LORD, from the ill and froward man
    give me deliverance,
  And do thou safe preserve me from
    the man of violence:
2 Who in their heart mischievous things
    are meditating ever;
  And they for war assembled are
    continually together.

3 Much like unto a serpent's tongue
    their tongues they sharp do make;
  And underneath their lips there lies
    the poison of a snake.
4 Lord, keep me from the wicked's hands,
    from vi'lent men me save;
  Who utterly to overthrow
    my goings purpos'd have.

5 The proud for me a snare have hid,
    and cords; yea, they a net
  Have by the way-side for me spread;
    they gins for me have set.

6   I said unto the Lord, Thou art
      my God: unto the cry
  Of all my supplications,
      Lord, do thine ear apply.

7   O God the Lord, who art the strength
      of my salvation:
  A cov'ring in the day of war
      my head thou hast put on.
8   Unto the wicked man, O Lord,
      his wishes do not grant;
  Nor further thou his ill device,
      lest they themselves should vaunt.

9   As for the head and chief of those
      about that compass me,
  Ev'n by the mischief of their lips
      let thou them cover'd be.
10 Let burning coals upon them fall,
      them throw in fiery flame,
  And in deep pits, that they no more
      may rise out of the same.

11 Let not an evil speaker be
      on earth established:
  Mischief shall hunt the vi'lent man,
      till he be ruined.
12 I know God will th' afflicted's cause
      maintain, and poor men's right.
13 Surely the just shall praise thy name;
      th' upright dwell in thy sight.

Psalm 141

A Psalm of David.

1 O LORD, I unto thee do cry,
    do thou make haste to me,
And give an ear unto my voice,
    when I cry unto thee.
2 As incense let my prayer be
    directed in thine eyes;
And the uplifting of my hands
    as th' ev'ning sacrifice.

3 Set, Lord, a watch before my mouth,
    keep of my lips the door.
4 My heart incline thou not unto
    the ills I should abhor,
To practise wicked works with men
    that work iniquity;
And with their delicates my taste
    let me not satisfy.

5 Let him that righteous is me smite,
    it shall a kindness be;
Let him reprove, I shall it count
    a precious oil to me:
Such smiting shall not break my head;
    for yet the time shall fall,
When I in their calamities
    to God pray for them shall.

6 When as their judges down shall be
    in stony places cast,
Then shall they hear my words; for they
    shall sweet be to their taste.

7 About the grave's devouring mouth
　　our bones are scatter'd round,
As wood which men do cut and cleave
　　lies scatter'd on the ground.

8 But unto thee, O God the Lord,
　　mine eyes uplifted be:
My soul do not leave destitute;
　　my trust is set on thee.
9 Lord, keep me safely from the snares
　　which they for me prepare;
And from the subtile gins of them
　　that wicked workers are.

10 Let workers of iniquity
　　into their own nets fall,
Whilst I do, by thine help, escape
　　the danger of them all.

Psalm 142

Maschil of David; A Prayer when he was in the cave.

1 I WITH my voice cry'd to the Lord,
　　with it made my request:
2 Pour'd out to him my plaint, to him
　　my trouble I exprest.
3 When in me was o'erwhelm'd my sp'rit,
　　then well thou knew'st my way;
Where I did walk a snare for me
　　they privily did lay.

4 I look'd on my right hand, and view'd,
　　but none to know me were;
All refuge failed me, no man
　　did for my soul take care.

5   I cry'd to thee; I said, Thou art
     my refuge, Lord, alone;
   And in the land of those that live
     thou art my portion.

6   Because I am brought very low,
     attend unto my cry:
   Me from my persecutors save,
     who stronger are than I.

7   From prison bring my soul, that I
     thy name may glorify:
   The just shall compass me, when thou
     with me deal'st bounteously.

Psalm 143

A Psalm of David.

1   LORD, hear my pray'r, attend my suits;
     and in thy faithfulness
   Give thou an answer unto me,
     and in thy righteousness.

2   Thy servant also bring thou not
     in judgment to be try'd:
   Because no living man can be
     in thy sight justify'd.

3   For th' en'my hath pursu'd my soul,
     my life to ground down tread:
   In darkness he hath made me dwell,
     as who have long been dead.

4   My sp'rit is therefore overwhelm'd
     in me perplexedly;
   Within me is my very heart
     amazed wondrously.

5   I call to mind the days of old,
      to meditate I use
On all thy works; upon the deeds
      I of thy hands do muse.

6   My hands to thee I stretch; my soul
      thirsts, as dry land, for thee.

7   Haste, Lord, to hear, my spirit fails:
      hide not thy face from me;

Lest like to them I do become
      that go down to the dust.

8   At morn let me thy kindness hear;
      for in thee do I trust.
Teach me the way that I should walk:
      I lift my soul to thee.

9   Lord, free me from my foes; I flee
      to thee to cover me.

10 Because thou art my God, to do
      thy will do me instruct:
Thy Sp'rit is good, me to the land
      of uprightness conduct.

11 Revive and quicken me, O Lord,
      ev'n for thine own name's sake;
And do thou, for thy righteousness,
      my soul from trouble take.

12 And of thy mercy slay my foes;
      let all destroyed be
That do afflict my soul: for I
      a servant am to thee.

Another of the same

1   OH, hear my prayer, Lord,
      And unto my desire

To bow thine ear accord,
  I humbly thee require;
And, in thy faithfulness,
  Unto me answer make,
And, in thy righteousness,
  Upon me pity take.

2 In judgment enter not
    With me thy servant poor;
  For why, this well I wot,
    No sinner can endure
  The sight of thee, O God:
    If thou his deeds shalt try,
  He dare make none abode
    Himself to justify.

3 Behold, the cruel foe
    Me persecutes with spite,
  My soul to overthrow:
    Yea, he my life down quite
  Unto the ground hath smote,
    And made me dwell full low
  In darkness, as forgot,
    Or men dead long ago.

4 Therefore my sp'rit much vex'd,
    O'erwhelm'd is me within;
  My heart right sore perplex'd
    And desolate hath been.
5 Yet I do call to mind
    What ancient days record,
  Thy works of ev'ry kind
    I think upon, O Lord.

6 Lo, I do stretch my hands
 To thee, my help alone;
For thou well understands
 All my complaint and moan:
My thirsting soul desires,
 And longeth after thee,
As thirsty ground requires
 With rain refresh'd to be.

7 Lord, let my pray'r prevail,
 To answer it make speed;
For, lo, my sp'rit doth fail:
 Hide not thy face in need;
Lest I be like to those
 That do in darkness sit,
Or him that downward goes
 Into the dreadful pit.

8 Because I trust in thee,
 O Lord, cause me to hear
Thy loving-kindness free,
 When morning doth appear:
Cause me to know the way
 Wherein my path should be;
For why, my soul on high
 I do lift up to thee.

9 From my fierce enemy
 In safety do me guide,
Because I flee to thee,
 Lord, that thou may'st me hide.
10 My God alone art thou,
 Teach me thy righteousness:

Thy Sp'rit's good, lead me to
The land of uprightness.

11 O Lord, for thy name's sake,
   Be pleas'd to quicken me;
And, for thy truth, forth take
   My soul from misery.
12 And of thy grace destroy
   My foes, and put to shame
All who my soul annoy;
   For I thy servant am.

Psalm 144

A Psalm of David.

1 O BLESSED ever be the Lord,
   who is my strength and might,
Who doth instruct my hands to war,
   my fingers teach to fight.
2 My goodness, fortress, my high tow'r,
   deliverer, and shield,
In whom I trust: who under me
   my people makes to yield.

3 Lord, what is man, that thou of him
   dost so much knowledge take?
Or son of man, that thou of him
   so great account dost make?
4 Man is like vanity; his days,
   as shadows, pass away.
5 Lord, bow thy heav'ns, come down, touch
                thou
   the hills, and smoke shall they.

6 Cast forth thy lightning, scatter them;
   thine arrows shoot, them rout.

7 Thine hand send from above, me save;
  from great depths draw me out;
And from the hand of children strange,
8   Whose mouth speaks vanity;
And their right hand is a right hand
  that works deceitfully.

9 A new song I to thee will sing,
  Lord, on a psaltery;
I on a ten-string'd instrument
  will praises sing to thee.
10 Ev'n he it is that unto kings
  salvation doth send;
Who his own servant David doth
  from hurtful sword defend.

11 O free me from strange children's hand,
  whose mouth speaks vanity;
And their right hand a right hand is
  that works deceitfully.
12 That, as the plants, our sons may be
  in youth grown up that are;
Our daughters like to corner-stones,
  carv'd like a palace fair.

13 That to afford all kind of store
  our garners may be fill'd;
That our sheep thousands, in our streets
  ten thousands they may yield.
14 That strong our oxen be for work,
  that no in-breaking be,
Nor going out; and that our streets
  may from complaints be free.

15 Those people blessed are who be
   in such a case as this;
   Yea, blessed all those people are,
   whose God JEHOVAH is.

Psalm 145

David's Psalm of praise.

1 I'LL thee extol, my God, O King;
   I'll bless thy name always.
2 Thee will I bless each day, and will
   thy name for ever praise.
3 Great is the Lord, much to be prais'd;
   his greatness search exceeds.
4 Race unto race shall praise thy works,
   and shew thy mighty deeds.

5 I of thy glorious majesty
   the honour will record;
   I'll speak of all thy mighty works,
   which wondrous are, O Lord.
6 Men of thine acts the might shall show,
   thine acts that dreadful are;
   And I, thy glory to advance,
   thy greatness will declare.

7 The mem'ry of thy goodness great
   they largely shall express;
   With songs of praise they shall extol
   thy perfect righteousness.
8 The Lord is very gracious,
   in him compassions flow;
   In mercy he is very great,
   and is to anger slow.

9   The Lord JEHOVAH unto all
     his goodness doth declare;
   And over all his other works
     his tender mercies are.
10 Thee all thy works shall praise, O Lord,
     and thee thy saints shall bless;
11 They shall thy kingdom's glory show,
     thy pow'r by speech express:

12 To make the sons of men to know
     his acts done mightily,
   And of his kingdom th' excellent
     and glorious majesty.
13 Thy kingdom shall for ever stand,
     thy reign through ages all.
14 God raiseth all that are bow'd down,
     upholdeth all that fall.

15 The eyes of all things wait on thee,
     the giver of all good;
   And thou, in time convenient,
     bestow'st on them their food:
16 Thine hand thou open'st lib'rally,
     and of thy bounty gives
   Enough to satisfy the need
     of ev'ry thing that lives.

17 The Lord is just in all his ways,
     holy in his works all.
18 God's near to all that call on him,
     in truth that on him call.
19 He will accomplish the desire
     of those that do him fear:

He also will deliver them,
    and he their cry will hear.

20 The Lord preserves all who him love,
      that nought can them annoy:
    But he all those that wicked are
      will utterly destroy.
21 My mouth the praises of the Lord
      to publish cease shall never:
    Let all flesh bless his holy name
      for ever and for ever.

Another of the same

1 O LORD, thou art my God and King;
      Thee will I magnify and praise:
    I will thee bless, and gladly sing
      Unto thy holy name always.
2 Each day I rise I will thee bless,
      And praise thy name time without end.
3 Much to be prais'd, and great God is;
      His greatness none can comprehend.

4 Race shall thy works praise unto race,
      The mighty acts show done by thee.
5 I will speak of the glorious grace,
      And honour of thy majesty;
    Thy wondrous works I will record.
6   By men the might shall be extoll'd
    Of all thy dreadful acts, O Lord:
      And I thy greatness will unfold.

7 They utter shall abundantly
      The mem'ry of thy goodness great;

And shall sing praises cheerfully,
    Whilst they thy righteousness relate.

8 The Lord our God is gracious,
    Compassionate is he also;
In mercy he is plenteous,
    But unto wrath and anger slow.

9 Good unto all men is the Lord:
    O'er all his works his mercy is.

10 Thy works all praise to thee afford:
    Thy saints, O Lord, thy name shall bless.

11 The glory of thy kingdom show
    Shall they, and of thy power tell;

12 That so men's sons his deeds may know,
    His kingdom's grace that doth excel.

13 Thy kingdom hath none end at all,
    It doth through ages all remain.

14 The Lord upholdeth all that fall,
    The cast-down raiseth up again.

15 The eyes of all things, Lord, attend,
    And on thee wait that here do live,
And thou, in season due, dost send
    Sufficient food them to relieve.

16 Yea, thou thine hand dost open wide,
    And ev'ry thing dost satisfy
That lives, and doth on earth abide,
    Of thy great liberality.

17 The Lord is just in his ways all,
    And holy in his works each one.

18 He's near to all that on him call,
    Who call in truth on him alone.

19 God will the just desire fulfil
    Of such as do him fear and dread:
  Their cry regard, and hear he will,
    And save them in the time of need.

20 The Lord preserves all, more and less,
    That bear to him a loving heart:
  But workers all of wickedness
    Destroy will he, and clean subvert.

21 Therefore my mouth and lips I'll frame
    To speak the praises of the Lord:
  To magnify his holy name
    For ever let all flesh accord.

Psalm 146

1 PRAISE God. The Lord praise, O my soul.
2 I'll praise God while I live;
  While I have being to my God
    in songs I'll praises give.
3 Trust not in princes, nor man's son,
    in whom there is no stay:
4 His breath departs, to's earth he turns;
    that day his thoughts decay.

5 O happy is that man and blest,
    whom Jacob's God doth aid;
  Whose hope upon the Lord doth rest,
    and on his God is stay'd:
6 Who made the earth and heavens high,
    who made the swelling deep,
  And all that is within the same;
    who truth doth ever keep:

7 Who righteous judgment executes
    for those oppress'd that be,

Who to the hungry giveth food;
   God sets the pris'ners free.
8 The Lord doth give the blind their sight,
   the bowed down doth raise:
The Lord doth dearly love all those
   that walk in upright ways.

9 The stranger's shield, the widow's stay,
   the orphan's help, is he:
But yet by him the wicked's way
   turn'd upside down shall be.
10 The Lord shall reign for evermore:
   thy God, O Sion, he
Reigns to all generations.
   Praise to the Lord give ye.

Psalm 147

1 PRAISE ye the Lord; for it is good
   praise to our God to sing:
For it is pleasant, and to praise
   it is a comely thing.
2 God doth build up Jerusalem;
   and he it is alone
That the dispers'd of Israel
   doth gather into one.

3 Those that are broken in their heart,
   and grieved in their minds,
He healeth, and their painful wounds
   he tenderly up-binds.
4 He counts the number of the stars;
   he names them ev'ry one.
5 Great is our Lord, and of great pow'r;
   his wisdom search can none.

6 The Lord lifts up the meek; and casts
  the wicked to the ground.
7 Sing to the Lord, and give him thanks;
  on harp his praises sound;
8 Who covereth the heav'n with clouds,
  who for the earth below
Prepareth rain, who maketh grass
  upon the mountains grow.

9 He gives the beast his food, he feeds
  the ravens young that cry.
10 His pleasure not in horses' strength,
  nor in man's legs, doth lie.
11 But in all those that do him fear
  the Lord doth pleasure take;
In those that to his mercy do
  by hope themselves betake.

12 The Lord praise, O Jerusalem;
  Sion, thy God confess:
13 For thy gates' bars he maketh strong;
  thy sons in thee doth bless.
14 He in thy borders maketh peace;
  with fine wheat filleth thee.
15 He sends forth his command on earth,
  his word runs speedily.

16 Hoar-frost, like ashes, scatt'reth he;
  like wool he snow doth give:
17 Like morsels casteth forth his ice;
  who in its cold can live?
18 He sendeth forth his mighty word,
  and melteth them again;

His wind he makes to blow, and then
  the waters flow amain.

19 The doctrine of his holy word
  to Jacob he doth show;
His statutes and his judgments he
  gives Israel to know.
20 To any nation never he
  such favour did afford;
For they his judgments have not known.
  O do ye praise the Lord.

Psalm *148*

1 PRAISE God. From heavens praise the
      Lord,
  in heights praise to him be.
2 All ye his angels, praise ye him;
  his hosts all, praise him ye.
3 O praise ye him, both sun and moon,
  praise him, all stars of light.
4 Ye heav'ns of heav'ns him praise, and floods
  above the heavens' height.

5 Let all the creatures praise the name
  of our almighty Lord:
For he commanded, and they were
  created by his word.
6 He also, for all times to come,
  hath them establish'd sure;
He hath appointed them a law,
  which ever shall endure.

7 Praise ye JEHOVAH from the earth,
  dragons, and ev'ry deep:

8 Fire, hail, snow, vapour, stormy wind,
    his word that fully keep.
9 All hills and mountains, fruitful trees,
    and all ye cedars high:
10 Beasts, and all cattle, creeping things,
    and all ye birds that fly.

11 Kings of the earth, all nations,
    princes, earth's judges all:
12 Both young men, yea, and maidens too,
    old men, and children small.
13 Let them God's name praise; for his name
    alone is excellent:
His glory reacheth far above
    the earth and firmament.

14 His people's horn, the praise of all
    his saints, exalteth he;
Ev'n Isr'el's seed, a people near
    to him. The Lord praise ye.

Another of the same

1 THE Lord of heav'n confess,
    On high his glory raise.
2 Him let all angels bless,
Him all his armies praise.
3   Him glorify
    Sun, moon, and stars;
4   Ye higher spheres,
    And cloudy sky.

5 From God your beings are,
Him therefore famous make;

You all created were,
When he the word but spake.
6 And from that place,
   Where fix'd you be
   By his decree,
   You cannot pass.

7 Praise God from earth below,
  Ye dragons, and ye deeps:
8 Fire, hail, clouds, wind, and snow,
  Whom in command he keeps.
9 Praise ye his name,
   Hills great and small,
   Trees low and tall;
10 Beasts wild and tame;

  All things that creep or fly.
11 Ye kings, ye vulgar throng,
  All princes mean or high;
12 Both men and virgins young,
   Ev'n young and old,
13 Exalt his name;
   For much his fame
   Should be extoll'd.

  O let God's name be prais'd
  Above both earth and sky;
14 For he his saints hath rais'd,
  And set their horn on high:
   Ev'n those that be
   Of Isr'el's race,
   Near to his grace.
   The Lord praise ye.

Psalm 149

1 PRAISE ye the Lord: unto him sing
   a new song, and his praise
  In the assembly of his saints
   in sweet psalms do ye raise.
2 Let Isr'el in his Maker joy,
   and to him praises sing:
  Let all that Sion's children are
   be joyful in their King.

3 O let them unto his great name
   give praises in the dance;
  Let them with timbrel and with harp
   in songs his praise advance.
4 For God doth pleasure take in those
   that his own people be;
  And he with his salvation
   the meek will beautify.

5 And in his glory excellent
   let all his saints rejoice:
  Let them to him upon their beds
   aloud lift up their voice.
6 Let in their mouth aloft be rais'd
   the high praise of the Lord,
  And let them have in their right hand
   a sharp two-edged sword;

7 To execute the vengeance due
   upon the heathen all,
  And make deserved punishment
   upon the people fall.

8   And ev'n with chains, as pris'ners, bind
     their kings that them command;
    Yea, and with iron fetters strong,
     the nobles of their land.

9   On them the judgment to perform
     found written in his word:
    This honour is to all his saints.
     O do ye praise the Lord.

Psalm 150

1   PRAISE ye the Lord. God's praise within
     his sanctuary raise;
    And to him in the firmament
     of his pow'r give ye praise.
2   Because of all his mighty acts,
     with praise him magnify:
    O praise him, as he doth excel
     in glorious majesty.

3   Praise him with trumpet's sound; his praise
     with psaltery advance:
4   With timbrel, harp, string'd instruments,
     and organs, in the dance.
5   Praise him on cymbals loud; him praise
     on cymbals sounding high.
6   Let each thing breathing praise the Lord.
     Praise to the Lord give ye.